Lon Chaney's
Shadow

JOHN JESKE AND THE CHANEY MYSTIQUE

by **Suzanne Gargiulo**

Lon Chaney's Shadow

John Jeske and the Chaney Mystique
©2009 Suzanne Gargiulo

Published in the USA by:

BearManor Media
P.O. Box 71426
Albany, Georgia 31708
www.BearManorMedia.com

ISBN-10: 1-59393-330-4 (alk. paper)

Book design and layout by Valerie Thompson

Table of Contents

Enlarged detail of production still from Chaney's last silent film *Thunder* **(1929, MGM) showing Lon Chaney and John Jeske (directly behind Chaney). Chaney became seriously ill while making this film in the bitter cold of Wisconsin and used Jeske as his stunt double.** (COURTESY OF THE ACADEMY OF MOTION PICTURE ARTS AND SCIENCES: MGM COLLECTION)

Introduction

Lon Chaney was the greatest actor Hollywood ever produced and a bona fide genius who single-handedly created the art of motion picture make-up. There was never anyone like him before or since, and I have an incredible amount of respect for his work and the honorable way he tried to live his life. In almost all of the books and articles I read about Chaney, I was struck by the repeated revelations of how he fiercely guarded his privacy and had very few close friends—friends who were carefully selected to be completely loyal to him and discreet. Chaney was no fool, and neither was his shrewd second wife, Hazel. Both could spot pretentious phonies miles away, and Chaney avoided all the hangers-on and "yes" men and women that seemed to swarm around motion picture stars like so many parasites. All that sort of thing sickened Chaney to his core, and he was only able to relax and enjoy the company of those who did not expect anything of him, or made unreasonable demands upon his time. The picture that formed in my mind of Chaney was not of someone who could be such an utterly poor judge of character that he would forge a close, personal bond with a "foreigner" who was nothing more than a greedy opportunist plotting to sleep with his wife behind his back and steal his money. That is the perception of John Fred Jeske given by Chaney's modern biographers, and it just doesn't fit the detailed profile of Chaney's obvious intelligence and intuitive ability in regards to assessing an individual's character.

I had to know who this John Jeske really was. How could Lon and Hazel Chaney have been so wrong about a man they claimed to be their "cherished and dependable friend"? I never imagined this search would be such a long and arduous one, nor did I think it would lead to another book. Even the most mundane details I thought would be so readily forthcoming have proven to be as elusive as the

Holy Grail. Jeske had no children, he wasn't close to his family, nearly everyone who would have known him is dead—the situation seemed bleak. Not all was lost, though, merely hidden under heavy layers of time. Through processing the information located from court documents, newspaper articles, census reports, voter registration records, historical maps, public and private collections, historical societies, ship's manifests, surviving Jeske family members, and the many individuals who have been so kind to offer whatever help they can, I have been able to reconstruct Jeske's life. In doing so, I came to the conclusion that John Jeske was a man who had, as Chaney wrote in his will two months before his death, "at all times been loyal" to the only true friends he had in the world—Lon and Hazel Chaney.

Jeske represents just one life out of the millions of lives that have nearly passed over into oblivion. His hopes and dreams, likes and dislikes, everything that made up the man he was has nearly faded away. Even his dead body was unceremoniously dumped into an unmarked grave that no one but the cemetery staff know is there. It took a lot of work to find him—so many phone calls to so many different cemeteries throughout the Los Angeles area. After researching the mortuary that handled the burial back in 1944, I located an article from the same time period about another man who died without a will or family to care about him. I was intrigued to learn he was buried in Inglewood. On a hunch, I called the Inglewood Park Cemetery and discovered that John Fred Jeske was indeed buried there.

Why should anyone really care, you may say? I wish I had the means to convey the urgency I feel about the need to tell John Jeske's true story for the very first time. Maybe it's my inherent love of justice, and the deep interest I have in the people I feel to have been wronged by history in some way. I believe Jeske is one of those people, and since there is no one left to pick up the gauntlet, I have taken on the very difficult task to attempt to set the record straight. Jeske had his faults, but he doesn't deserve the harsh indictment of his character that is presented in the precious little of his life story that survives today. I, for one, have grown to care about this forgotten man, and I honestly feel that all who read this book with an open mind and heart will too.

The full chronicle of the events of John Jeske's life and amazing career as Chaney's chauffeur, assistant, companion, confidant, and "man of all jobs," is full of sharp twists and turns and, ultimately, tragedy. I couldn't help but be affected by the sadness surrounding Chaney's early death at age 47 in 1930, and Hazel's collapse at his funeral where her soul-searing cries of "Why? Why?" reverberated throughout the church. The emotional pain of Creighton Chaney's love-hate relationship with his father that fuelled his descent into alcoholism also touched me. What caused him to be so distant from his step-mother after his father died, and why did Hazel feel the need to protect herself from the Chaney family to such an extreme that she contemplated marrying Jeske? Some of these questions I can provide an answer to, but so many others will never truthfully be known. There are conflicting accounts that further muddy the already murky waters, and at this late date one can only sift through the remaining evidence and make up their own minds as to what really happened.

Jeske appears to have been a pawn in the game being played by the son and his step-mother, and ended up an easy target for vicious rumors and ridicule. After all, this was a time in America—the early 1930s—when a person of German heritage was often vilified for all the damage done by Germany during World War I, and the fear growing out of the looming malevolence of Adolph Hitler and his Third Reich. With his German background and noticeable accent, Jeske was especially hated by Creighton Chaney, who had an obsessive dislike of all "foreigners." The confused and bizarre events that occurred around the time of Hazel's death in 1933 only fanned the flames of hatred already present in Creighton's heart, and the fact that Jeske was to receive $25,000 from his father's estate and yet Hazel had effectively disinherited him, was the last straw. The story of what followed the reading of Hazel's will, and the incredible series of events over the course of the next eight months would culminate in the kidnapping and robbery of Jeske and his new bride by thugs who had inside information regarding Jeske's relationship to Hazel Chaney. When the kidnappers were finally apprehended after the Jeske's suffered a harrowing two-week ordeal, Jeske told the Sheriff that one of the kidnappers was a relative of Lon Chaney's first wife—Creighton Chaney's mother. Could Creighton's hatred of

Jeske have escalated to the point of setting Jeske up for the crime in order to get back the inheritance he believed to be rightfully his? There is tantalizing evidence of his involvement, but such an act seems almost too vicious to be believed. Perhaps, it's more a matter of not wanting to believe it could be true.

The theme that kept repeating itself over and over again as I researched this subject was abject tragedy. Lon Chaney died with so many things left undone in his life—the beautiful new house he would never enjoy, the new cabin in the mountains he was so looking forward to relaxing in, the two little grandsons he would never teach how to choose that perfect fly and cast a rod. He didn't want to leave this world so soon, and he feared for what would happen to Hazel. Chaney had a good reason to worry, for she was never to recover from the loss of her husband and succumbed to cancer only three years later. And what of John Jeske? His life, too, would end in sadness, disappointment, and an early death three days after his 54th birthday. Yet the life he led during those ten years he spent with the Chaney's were filled with a lot of happiness and personal discovery, and the details of these amazing times—along with the rest of Jeske's complex life—should be accurately recorded, remembered, and impartially evaluated.

One can focus on Lon Chaney's many achievements as a phenomenally talented actor and pioneering make-up artist to the exclusion of all else, but I feel we are doing him a great disservice to neglect his human side. I believe I have been able to locate enough material to give a clear, accurate picture of what happened during the days of Chaney and Jeske, including some personal recollections from friends and colleagues. I firmly believe the fascinating details of Lon Chaney's final years, along with the story of Jeske's complex life, should be accurately recorded, remembered, and impartially evaluated. Nothing can diminish Chaney's cinematic legacy. This book will only serve to flesh out the skeleton of a story heretofore provided of Chaney's life and shed more light on the Chaney mystique and the man who knew its secrets—John Jeske.

Acknowledgments

So many kind people helped me with this very difficult project. I know I will forget to mention someone, and I apologize in advance for any oversight. I would first like to thank the tireless researchers who did some of the more treacherous legwork for me through the Los Angeles County court system and beyond to locate and copy invaluable documents: Charlene Dodenhoff Patterson, Christina McKillip, Debra L. Wiley, Ted Gostin, and George Fogelson. The frustrating, time-consuming process of locating the necessary documents could fill another volume in itself, complete with tales of disappearing files and melted microfilm in a locked security vault.

A very special "thank you" goes to Kenneth Partridge for his kindness and first-hand account of John Jeske as he knew him. I also can't thank Robert Jeske and his wife Ruth enough for their kindness and helpfulness throughout this project. The book would not have been possible without Bob's insight into the Jeske familiy history. I was saddened by his passing in February of 2007. May he rest in peace. Alice (Jeske: Sadly, Alice passed away in 2006) and George Brink, Debbie Davis, Freda (Jeske) Hollenback (who passed away in 2005), Laura Anderson, Laurin Peterlin, Babe (Rossi) Harwood, Duane Rossi, Jeanne Stewart (Glacier Pack Train Station, Big Pine), Janie Hunstberger, Richard Huntstberger, George (Ted) Huntsberger, and Philip J. Riley also provided invaluable information and help.

Many thanks also go out to the following individuals, listed in no special order, for everything they did to make this book a reality:

Chris Langley, Inyo County Film Commission

Linda Reynolds and Trudy Garza, Inyo National Forest

Joe Bryer, Geneological Research Society of NE PA

Barbara Smith and Delores McKinney, Brentwood Historical Society

Nancy O'Neill, Santa Monica Public Library

Dace Taube, Specialized Libraries and Archival Collections, University of Southern California

Simon Elliott, UCLA Special Collections Library

Carolyn Kozo Cole, Curator of Photographs, Los Angeles Public Library

Faye Thompson, Photo Archives, and Kristine Krueger, NFIS, Margaret Herrick Library, Academy of Motion Picture Arts and Sciences

Randy Thompson, NARA-Pacific Region

Norma Reese, Forest Hill Cemetery Association

Fran Bumann, So Cal Genealogical Society & Family Research Center

T. Maureen Schoenky, Germanic Research, SCGS

Karen Krugman, Detroit Society of Genealogical Research

Joan R. Shanahan, Inglewood Park Cemetery

Marsha Grigsby, Los Angeles County Coroner's office

Steve Lawson, Humanities Librarian, Colorado College

Genevieve Troka, Caifornia State Archives

Elena Tsvetkova and Kristin Nute, Blitz Information Center

Melvin Ashmon, California Court of Appeal (2nd Appellate)

I am grateful to Kevin Brownlow and Marc Wanamaker for being kind enough to listen and offer their advice even though they had no information to further my research. I appreciated the fact that both Michael Blake and Ron Chaney, Jr. cordially responded to my inquiries regardless of their bias against Jeske. Donna Halper, Ralph Beattie, Jim Beattie, and Helene Demeestere were also helpful. Thank you to Robert Whiteman of Liberty Library Corp, who is collecting all the Hollywood stories from *Liberty Magazine* for publication in one book.

Last but certainly not least, I would like to thank my patient husband Robert Rutherford, my brother Shane Gargiulo, and my good friends for their support and encouragement. I could not have completed this book without their love and my faith in God through Jesus Christ.

Foreword

"I'll fix it so that no one will ever write my life story."
— *Lon Chaney, circa 1928*

I've often wondered if he meant that quote or was he using secrecy about his personal life as a publicity stunt. The effect being that the public was even more curious for the unknown facts.

After having the world's largest archive on Chaney at one time—having read the diaries of his first wife, Cleva, interviewed his son, cousin, brother, and others close to him—I found that there surely wasn't anything that would shock anyone by today's morals and standards. But in the 1920s and 1930s, the stories definitely would have affected his career. At the time of his death he was the number one box office attraction in the world. Like many people who climb to the top of their profession, his family did suffer the worst side of his personality.

Chaney always had one close friend in his life. All much younger mentors like George Loane Tucker, Irving Thalberg, Carl Laemmle, Jr. He and his second wife Hazel's circle of friends were all from different walks of life—lawyers, military men, sportsmen, professional fighters. Because the general population knew him as his screen characters—The Phantom of the Opera or the Hunchback of Notre Dame; the vampire from the lost film *London After Midnight*; clowns, and scarred villains—he could usually go just about anywhere in public and not be recognized. Throughout his film career from pre-1915 Universal Pictures to being a star at MGM, his wife Hazel seems to have been his best friend and companion. I say this because everything points to Chaney, (never a forgiving man), as having remained deeply in turmoil over the love/hate relationship with his first wife, Cleva.

Of all the people in Chaney's life there was one person who completely eluded me. I could never discover how John Jeske, handyman, driver, makeup assistant, personal assistant, figured so prominently in Chaney's life during the brief six years he was a major star. I checked public and private records and it was all fascinating reading—almost like a Dashiell Hammett novel—but I was left with more questions than answers. Why was he one of the few who were allowed in Chaney's makeup room? Jeske bought his makeup and helped apply it in areas Chaney could not reach by himself. Why was he permitted to act as Chaney's stand-in in the last half dozen pictures Chaney made for MGM studios?

And the biggest questions came after Chaney's death. Why was he hated by the remaining Chaney family after Lon Chaney's untimely death in 1930? Jeske and Hazel were the last persons to see him alive, aside from the hospital staff. Why was he mentioned—called a "faithful servant"—in Chaney's will while Lon Chaney, Jr. only received a small amount of insurance money? Why did Hazel refuse Louis B Mayer's attempt to get the $50,000 bonus given to Chaney for his next talkie *The Bugle Sounds*? And what followed in the next three years is amazing: Manipulations of the money left by Chaney, cutting off of Chaney's lawyer Milton Cohen to be replaced by attorney Claude Parker, Jeske's attempt to marry Hazel Chaney on her deathbed, missing jewelry, and finally Jeske himself being kidnapped. These are events which completely eluded me in thirty-five years of studying Lon Chaney. People still love his screen characters, which have never been topped even by today's computer generated special effects. However, it is important to all fans and historians to know what drives a man to reach such heights—the events in his life that made his professional life possible. Personal information on any public figure is so very essential to all to learn how to improve our own lives. And now for the first time Suzanne Gargiulo has painstakingly researched and unimpeachable documented the relationship between one the silent screen's greatest reclusive stars, Lon Chaney, and his best companion and friend, John Jeske.

For me, knowing the real true life story of Lon Chaney, this book answers the last of the mysteries for me and it reveals a personal look into the final years of his life.

"Between pictures there is no Lon Chaney"

PHILIP J RILEY

JANUARY 13, 2009

Chapter 1:

NEW BEGINNINGS AND GLIMPSES OF THE PAST

What a thrilling era to be alive! The economy was booming, the ugly war that divided the globe was over and prosperity was everywhere in this new golden age. The year 1923 was especially bright for the citizens of that magical place—Hollywood, California. The infant motion picture industry had grown into a thriving, hungry animal that was feeding on the hopes and dreams of a star-struck world. Immigrants from all over the world were pouring into the city looking for a chance to make their mark, and many did find success. Films were then a silent medium that didn't discriminate against those with only a meager grasp of the English language. It was a relatively level playing field, and the players were never in short supply. Times were indeed very good for those with a little talent and a willingness to work hard.

On a sunny day in the early part of 1923—we can assume it was sunny since so many Californian days are—one such immigrant arose early to start his work day like always with the usual routine. However, this was not to be just a routine day for John Friedrich Jeske, nor would any of the days to follow. But for now, he merely straightens up the spartan room he rents at the boarding house on South Flower Street and prepares himself for the day ahead. As he busies himself in front of the mirror, we see a reflection of a relatively young man of thirty with a strong jaw line and mischievous black eyes; a rather handsome reflection. Jeske preened and fussed with his thinning dark brown hair until he had achieved just the right look. He could never be sure when he may run into that pretty young lady, Adele, who rented the room a couple of doors down. She was single like he was, and perhaps she was looking for a little fun. The situation never seemed right, though, to ask her out, and his empty pockets made trying to impress Adele impossible at the moment. The sound of her name evoked memories of the sister he left behind when he boarded the ship in Hamburg to come to America back in 1912. So much had changed since then.

"John" seemed like a good, nondescript, American name, Jeske thought. He took the name shortly after his arrival in the United States to diffuse the anti-German sentiment that was still very much alive in this country. He was born in what was formerly the Polish city of Skierniewice to a German father and Polish mother. It was spring in this bustling city not far from the metropolis of Lödz when Friedrich Jeske was born on May 7, 1890. The family was not wealthy, and they seemed to be frequently on the move. Due to his father's German ancestry, the family members were considered hostile "aliens" in a land then controlled by Russia. The inhabitants of what was once the proud country of Poland were placed under heavy pressure to become assimilated into Russian culture and forget their own past. Ludwig Jeske and his wife Julia Martin (a more ethnically neutral version of her birth name, Juliana Martsinkovski) raised nine children: Gustav, Julius, Carl, Friedrich, Amelia, Anna, Otelia, Olga, and Adele.[1] The Jeske family spoke both German and Polish at home, and would have had to be fairly fluent in Russian as well to conduct official government business.

By 1912, all four of the Jeske brothers had left Europe and landed either in New York or Baltimore on their way to Scranton, Pennsylvania. Julius Jeske arrived first in 1905 and established himself in this working-class mining town by opening his own bakery. Julius and his cousin Christina Krieg married in 1906 (a few months after her boat docked in New York), and they quickly began to build a family. Gustav and Carl arrived in June of 1906 from Bremen, Germany, to join Julius and his new wife. By 1911, all three brothers, Christina, and several children co-existed in the small home above the bakery on Pittston Avenue. Julius and Carl ran the bakery together with Gustav—or "Gus" as he was known—providing the backbone of the business. The following year, with a war brewing in Europe and fears for his brother's safety, Carl sent his younger brother Friedrich the money to buy passage to America.

Details of Friedrich's life prior to his arrival in the New World are sketchy at best, but the place where he lived and worked tells quite a bit about what the conditions must have been like. Friedrich lived in the company town of Herrenwyk in Germany, located about 40 miles northeast of Hamburg. The town was built and maintained for the workers of the metal-, employing hundreds of workers until the factory's demise in the early 1980s. Herrenwyk could not survive after the factory closed down, and what is left of it is now preserved as a museum. The work at the factory must have been strenuous and the hours long, but a strong young man of 20 could manage the hardships a little easier than most. Descriptions of the factory's huge blast furnace evoke images of a demonic beast constantly demanding a human sacrifice. The conditions in the factory were unbearable at times due to the high heat and dust.[2]

Friedrich was probably eager to leave the harsh life in Herrenwyk behind and join his brothers in America. The growing unrest throughout Europe made the prospects of a major war more of a reality, and Ludwig Jeske may have wanted to see that his sons all made it safely to America before the trouble came. Friedrich arrived in Hamburg in early March of 1912 to board the *Batavia*, which was bound for New York. After boarding the ship and supplying the clerk with all the necessary information for the ship's manifest, Friedrich inexplicably disembarks and didn't sail with the *Batavia* when she left port on March 9th. With his destination in the U.S. being Pennsylvania, possibly some deep seated superstition compelled him to wait until the 23rd to sail so that he could be aboard the *S.S. Pennsylvania*. This huge ship carried over 2,700 passengers—the majority of whom roughed it in their third-class accommodations.[3] This was Friedrich's first ocean voyage, and though he was a now a young man of 21, he took a boyish delight in all the new sights and sounds. He had never been content with the societal limitations placed upon his life, and he yearned for the freedom to express his true self. The weather was a little uncooperative, and the *Pennsylvania* was delayed by a few days in docking. Upon its arrival in New York on April 5th, a weary but excited Friedrich rushed down the gangway to the smiling faces and warm hugs of brothers Carl and Gustav, who whisked their little brother on a train back to Scranton.

The atmosphere at Julius Jeske's home was probably not what a young bachelor like Friedrich was expecting, and he had to quickly adjust himself to the hustle and bustle and little children everywhere. Julius was a very strong-willed, impetuous man who was used to getting his own way. By now Julius and Christina had three children—Julius Jr., Caroline, and Elizabeth. Gustav, a year older than Julius, was a mild-mannered bachelor also living at the home. Not long after Friedrich's arrival, Carl decided to try his luck in Detroit, Michigan. His relationship with Julius had soured considerably, and his baking skills were not especially keen. The final straw had been an attempt to become a partner in Julius' bakery, which was renamed the Jeske Brothers Bakery.[4] Personal and professional pressures mounted quickly and forced an early retreat from Carl, who couldn't stand another day under his older brother's thumb. In Detroit, Carl left Scranton behind him, as well as the turmoil of his family. He was heard from sporadically through letters to his nieces, especially the youngest ones, Emma and Freda. His concern for their welfare was genuine and his letters revealed a gentle and generous nature. Carl found a little comfort in the home of a widowed German woman he rented a room from on Navahoe Street, and he struggled to find work as a carpenter. Carl was able to obtain contracts with the government for various building projects that kept him quite well off for the time. His short and unremarkable life ended at the age of 47 on November 10, 1936 when he slipped and fell from the home's second-story balcony and suffered a severe head fracture.[5] Like his brother Gustav, he neither married nor had children. Another life—out of millions of lives—that ultimately slips through the cracks of history.

Julius' growing family and growing problems with alcohol caused a rift with his youngest brother Friedrich as well. The differences between them would prove to be an insurmountable chasm. Gustav seemed to bear all with a fatalistic sort of resignation that neither questioned the circumstances he found himself in, nor asked for any better. He and his little brother Friedrich had a close bond that somehow survived all the changes to come. As the year 1914 approached, John—as Friedrich was calling himself now—was already tired of doing odd jobs for Julius in the bakery and dealing with the crowding, noise, and smells of a houseful of children. He was dreaming of a better life in this land of opportunity—a place where he could carve out a niche for himself. Ours is a society that is fixated on the trappings of success—big houses, big bank accounts, fancy cars, jewelry, and other expensive baubles. Jeske wasn't about to let his lack of education get in the way of achieving the sort of material success he knew would bring the respect and admiration he craved. He was tired of living in poverty and always just barely scraping by, but what could he do?

By the end of 1914, Jeske made the decision to cut ties with his family in Scranton and head out west to the warm climate of California. Here was a place where fortunes were being made and dreams fulfilled, or so it seemed to an unworldly young man like Jeske. He wasn't sure what he was going to do when he got there, but he knew it was going to be something spectacular.

Jeske arrived in Los Angeles sometime in November when the air had a bit of a chill to it. For someone who had survived the harsh winters of Eastern Europe and Scranton, the cold was barely noticeable. It was the lack of English skills and *savoir faire* that caused the most trouble at first. Fortunately, he had been blessed with an innate charm and flair to his personality which helped to smooth over any rough spots. Jeske was able to find a small room he could afford in an undistinguished part of the downtown area and looked for work. He had a fascination with automobiles and loved to tinker with them any chance he could get. Neither Jeske nor his family had enough money to buy one, but that didn't stop him from fantasizing about being behind the wheel of some impressive machine. It seemed a perfect fit, then, when Jeske was able to find a job driving a car for a local taxi company. Jeske proudly referred to himself now as a "chauffeur" and enjoyed his new vocation, though in the back of his mind he knew he was destined for better things. There seemed to be a certain restless quality about him—a sense of pent-up energy waiting to be released—that never quite allowed him to become comfortable for long, and he had a series of menial jobs before landing anything really secure. Jeske had an artistic temperament, and a large amount of skill to match, that he often used to amuse himself and others. One thing was certain, though—he wanted to remain in this new land and become a full citizen. On April 8, 1920, he drove down to the courthouse to file the necessary Declaration of Intention to begin the long process towards citizenship.

The job Jeske was headed to on that sunny day in 1923 was probably the most promising he had landed yet. He was employed as an auto operator for a small auto repair garage near Hollywood, and there was a chance for advancement. A mechanic who worked alongside Jeske, and who quickly became a close friend, was a man of German-French ancestry named Louis Mansey. Mansey had recently arrived in Los Angeles with his wife Ona from Wyoming, where he had worked at Yellowstone National Park. He had been born and raised in Montana, and sort of "drifted away" during the late teens to explore life on his own.[6] Mansey was an expert mechanic, and dreamed of the day when he could own the repair shop himself. The shop had an excellent reputation around town for crack mechanics, and the lure of top-notch service brought in serious auto aficionados like actor Lon Chaney.

Chaney's star was rapidly on the rise, and he was on the verge of fulfilling one of his most cherished ambitions—bringing Victor Hugo's *The Hunchback of Notre Dame* to the screen in a big-budget extravaganza befitting of such a tale. In 1923, the 40-year-old actor was a ruggedly handsome, virile man with piercing deep-set eyes that seemed always to be probing and questioning. Though tamed a bit by age and experience, Chaney still possessed some of the nervous, high-strung, and volatile qualities he had exhibited in his younger days.[7] His movements were quick and agile—his manner friendly but somewhat wary. Chaney once told an acquaintance he could size a person up within sixty seconds and immediately form a full personality profile just by studying certain aspects of their physical appearance. If after one minute Chaney approved of you— you were in solid. If he found something in your looks that told him you were no good—nothing on this earth could ever make him think otherwise.[8] Chaney—by more than one account—could be a "hard man," at times unforgiving and harsh. Yet, as is the way with all complex human beings, he could also be extremely gentle and compassionate—especially toward those he felt were somehow misunderstood by society or misjudged in some way. And for the mere handful of individuals who could lay claim to being Chaney's friend; Chaney would lower his formidable internal defenses and share a little of his true self. Loyalty, faithfulness, and friendship were of paramount importance to Chaney, who was beginning in 1923 to see the negative side of celebrity. The greater the amount of fame he won with his acting and make-up skills, the more the public seemed to crave intimate details of his private life. With more than a few things he wished to keep buried about his past, Chaney would become increasingly reticent.

Prior to 1923, Chaney had often appeared on the movie set like a little boy eager to show off a new toy when he was approached by a journalist asking about his acting work and make-up techniques. He made no secret about his ambition to "become the greatest character man and heavy on the screen," and enjoyed talking about how he meticulously developed and researched his characters.[9] By early 1923, with his greatest work yet looming on the horizon, Chaney began a very calculated and systematic effort to erase Lon Chaney, the man, from the public landscape. He confided part of the plan to *Los Angeles Times* reporter Hallet Abend: "Lately, I have bought every old plate and negative that shows me without make-up. I think it's best to be anonymous; to veil my individuality behind the parts I play."[10] The culmination of this disappearing act for the "real" Lon Chaney would be the release of his most ambitious make-up work ever attempted—a complete transformation of face and body meant to obliterate anything that would betray his recognizable features. It was this stroke of creative genius—Chaney's "Quasimodo" from *The Hunchback of Notre Dame*—that would forever alter Chaney both as an artist and as a man. It was also the catalyst that brought him and struggling immigrant John Jeske together.

It is interesting to wonder if anyone had ever told Jeske prior to his first meeting with the actor in 1923 of his strong resemblance to Chaney. Whether Jeske was aware of it or not, the truth was that both men were roughly the same height and weight, with similar deep lines on their cheeks and deep-set, vibrant eyes that were so dark they appeared black.[11] Chaney certainly must have noticed the similarity the moment he drove his car into the garage that fateful day to be serviced by his buddy Louis Mansey. Mansey and Chaney both shared a love of the outdoors and automobiles, and they liked to trade stories about their fishing trips and mountain adventures.

Chaney wanted to know who the new guy was, and Mansey called Jeske over and introduced the two men. Jeske must have easily passed the "sixty-second" test, for Chaney quickly became enthralled with this younger doppelganger. In one of those serendipitous moments of inspiration, Chaney began to devise a way to make good use of Jeske's untapped skills.

Chaney was feeling the pressure to make a box-office success out of *Hunchback*. For the first time in his career, he was given the opportunity to not only pitch his own particular project idea, but participate in choosing the director, his co-stars, how the screenplay was to be fashioned, and nearly every other aspect of the production. It was extremely important to Chaney to do it all his own way with very little interference from the bigwigs at Universal Studios, or even his hand-picked director, Wallace Worsely. The make-up and costumes he designed for the role of the hunchback Quasimodo were so cumbersome and elaborate that Chaney knew he was going to need help to put it all together. Still, he felt it necessary that the details of his revolutionary techniques be kept absolutely secret. Chaney's ego—which he denied gratifying in so many other ways—now demanded to be fed due to the extreme pride he felt at his achievement. He couldn't resist asking a few select journalists to enter his dressing room to witness the early stages of the nearly three-hour procedure to transform himself into the character. When it came time to prepare the more elaborate prosthetics and specially designed body harness and rubber suit to complete his amazing transformation, he would order everyone out of his dressing room and lock the door. Not quite everyone, though.[12]

Besides the desire for secrecy, Chaney also wanted to hide the fact he had to resort to the use of several assistants to help with the creation and application of his full body costume, which included the heavy plaster "hump," wig and other make-up devices. Chaney strongly desired to be seen as just a regular guy who didn't let all the glitz and glamour of Hollywood go to his head. He openly sneered at other top actors who arrived at the studios with their entourages, and angrily denied his need for a valet or any other kind of assistant.[13] With such a well-publicized stand on the subject, it was a little awkward to say the least for Chaney to think of showing up at the studio one day with his own private dresser and make-up assistant. This wasn't the first time he had needed help with a costume—as the legless crime lord "Blizzard" from *The Penalty* (1920), Chaney required help fitting himself with a leather harness he devised to strap his legs behind his back—but with the need to improve and expand on all his earlier make-up triumphs, he would be needing more help on a regular basis.

Chaney decided to hire Jeske as his assistant, but had to figure out a way to slip him into his dressing room without anyone realizing what he was doing there. Seeing Jeske that day at the auto repair garage provided Chaney with the perfect solution—hire Jeske as the family chauffeur. Since Jeske had worked as a driver for a taxicab company, and now drove cars for the garage, being a private chauffeur was an easy transition to make. This seemed like the perfect cover; even though it was obvious to anyone who really knew Chaney that he preferred to be behind the wheel and didn't need a chauffeur. Neither did Mrs. Chaney—the former Hazel Bennett Hastings—who had been managing just fine for eight years without a driver. Still, a chauffeur would boost their stock quite a bit in the eyes of their neighbors, and Hazel felt it was high time they enjoyed some of the perks of her husband's position. A frugal woman by nature, and an extremely shrewd businesswoman who handled most of the financial decisions, Hazel viewed her marriage to Chaney in some ways as if it were an investment she fully intended to pay off big in the long run. Both partners had suffered from unhappy first marriages: Lon's nearly eight-year marriage to Frances "Cleva" Creighton had produced one son, Creighton in 1906. Hazel had been married to a legless man who sold cigars and tickets at the theatre where she was working in her hometown of San Francisco.

When Lon first met her in 1905, Cleva Creighton was a tall, idealistic, girl of sixteen living in Oklahoma City who dreamt of one day becoming a great dancer. Against her mother's wishes, she left home to join a traveling theatre company that had advertised in the local paper for new chorus girls. Cleva's heart melted when she answered the ad and saw her handsome young dancing instructor, Lon Chaney (who was a naturally gifted dancer and choreographer). As Cleva put it many years later, "My heart took wings and flew right to him."[14] Though she was a terrible dancer, she was blessed with a beautiful singing voice that spoke to Chaney's profound love of music. A more earthy love quickly blossomed between Cleva and her eager mentor, and soon the two were sharing a bed. Chaney wasn't completely naïve about life, but he had never before opened his heart like he had with this young girl. Before long, Cleva discovered she was pregnant, and her dreams of fame and fortune were suddenly snuffed out. Chaney must have been in a daze, not knowing what to do next and worrying about what the future would bring. He had been raised to be an honorable man, and he knew he couldn't abandon Cleva and his unborn child, but this was the last thing he wanted. With very little money and no personal support of any real kind on the road, the couple was forced to return to Oklahoma City in order for Cleva to be near her mother. Lon would put his theatrical career on hold to take a "regular" job in a furniture store to make ends meet. His early training as a carpet layer and wallpaper hanger would serve him well.

Cleva's mother Mattie was not pleased at all by this turn of events. She was already angry that Cleva defied her and went away with what she felt to be a sleazy traveling show, but now her daughter returns home pregnant by one of the actors! A good mother couldn't refuse her child in a time of need, and Cleva certainly needed help with what was turning out to be a difficult pregnancy. The young girl was feeling weak and sick, requiring almost constant bedrest. Though Mattie did what she could to help her daughter, she made her objections known when she decided not to attend Lon and Cleva's modest wedding on May 31, 1906. Possibly, the fact that the young couple's baby boy—Creighton Tull Chaney—was already three months old by the time of the marriage influenced her actions.[15] As soon as Cleva and the baby—who was born premature and nearly died from lack of oxygen—were strong enough, Lon quit his job at the furniture store and they all headed out to join up with the traveling theatre company once again.

The marriage quickly stagnated and began to disintegrate as the pressures of caring for a small child and working nearly seven days a week took its toll. The constant moving from town to town and frequent bouts of abject poverty were proving too much for Cleva. She found relief in the various outside singing jobs she was able to find at bars and cabarets. Cleva had an appealing, sensuous style that helped her achieve a certain measure of success—more than her hard-working husband at the time. While supportive at first due to the extra money Cleva's jobs brought in, Chaney's hot temper, made even more volatile by the chronic lack of sleep, food, funds, and overwork, soon boiled over at the double insult of Cleva becoming more famous than he was, and that his wife was required to get chummy with the male customers. For Cleva, it was refreshing to be able to sit down with a man after a performance, have a drink, and just talk. How she craved that little gesture of acknowledgment that reminded her she was a human being—a woman. Lon rarely paid attention to her anymore, and it seemed like he didn't have time to be a real husband to her since the birth of Creighton and their frenetic life on the road. Lon was always kind to her, but he moved about as if he were in a world all his own, save for the moments that he spent with his beloved baby boy. What happened to *her* life? Somehow this sense of dissatisfaction made it easier for Cleva to forget about Lon—even Creighton—for a few moments while she had a drink or two with a man who at least *pretended* to care about her feelings. She became so wrapped up in this other life that she found herself writing a letter to one of the bartenders who listened to her troubles and seemed so full of compassion. The letter ended with "Yours, all the time with love, Cleva."[16] It was very unfortunate indeed that Lon found the letter before Cleva had a chance to mail it. Loyalty, faithfulness, and friendship—everything he held dear had been blown apart by the revelation his own Cleva could be cheating on him. Her increasing dependence on alcohol was bad enough, but now this. Lon's trust had been betrayed and there was no going back. The hard, unyielding, unmerciful part of his nature was aroused to its fullest. Nothing Cleva could say or do could change Lon's mind—he wanted nothing more to do with her. A distraught Cleva's ill-conceived, and very public, suicide attempt on April 30, 1913 at the Majestic Theatre in Los Angeles did nothing but convince Lon she was an unfit mother for his son. They permanently separated as of May 26th, and little Creighton temporarily was allowed to stay with his mother. On December 13th, Lon filed for a divorce and full custody of his son. The divorce hearing was held on April 1, 1914—Lon's 31st birthday—and the judgment was easily granted in his favor both for the divorce from Cleva and custody of their son Creighton, since Cleva did not appear to defend herself.[17] She did send a letter to Chaney that was entered into the court record pleading for a chance to see her son: "Don't think I am going to ask for forgiveness. I want permission to see our boy. I have paid and am still paying dearly for it. But you don't care and I can't expect even a word from you; but for God's sake grant my only hold to the name of Chaney, and let me see my dear baby. I would be a slave or anything else just to see him. I promise I will not beg your forgiveness or harm you in any way. I know, Lon, that you loved me once, and to think I am not worthy of that love. Lon, I am almost crazy. Please return good for evil once more as you have always done with me." Years later she would say that she knew she had been wrong and said, "I don't think I realized then that my boy was gone for good. I was so ill and miserable and I hated myself so. . . . Lon meant well, but he shouldn't have hated me like he did. I've paid for being an ignorant fool."

The sad irony is that Cleva, even after she remarried years later, always loved Lon, and claimed to have never felt any malice toward him for what happened.[18] The girl who was the first to warm Lon's young heart had now turned it stone cold—he refused to even say her name again until shortly before he died.

As a child of divorce who spent his formative years in chaotic and sometimes hostile environments, Creighton bore the emotional and psychological scars of his troubled upbringing. To his credit, Lon did everything he possibly could to make sure his son was fed, clothed (he even made the boy's clothing), and well cared for. There are many stories of the great personal sacrifices Chaney made to keep his sad little family together. For a dozen years his whole life had revolved around the theatre—as stagehand and manager, wardrobe "mistress," choreographer, make-up man, performer of comedy and dancing parts—nearly twenty-four hours a day, seven days a week. Even with all this work, he would frequently end up with no money to show for his trouble. An especially poignant image that survives from those early days is of an exhausted Chaney, who had finished a day of three or four grueling shows, going out into the night to do his "eccentric" dance routine in front of a local bar in order to collect the few coins that will allow him to buy some food for his hungry family. Creighton wasn't the only one to be forever marked by these bleak and seemingly hopeless days. The sting of Cleva's betrayal would forever haunt him and play a pivotal role in altering the entire course of his life. Cleva too was forever changed: The poison she took in an attempt to end her life damaged her vocal chords. She couldn't sing a note and lost what little chance she had at a better life. Lon's bitterness was so deep he told Creighton his mother was dead, and did everything possible to see to it that Cleva would never see her son again.[19] To complete the plan, Lon sought to erase every connection to this marriage from his life, with the exception of Creighton, who found himself living in what amounted to foster homes while his father struggled to get back on his feet.

The tragedy of Chaney's early marriage had an unexpected positive effect on his career. The scandal of Cleva's suicide attempt in 1913 and the divorce were instrumental in the decision by Chaney's employers—the successful comedic duo of Kolb & Dill—to fire Chaney. Desperate to find stable work, Chaney heeded the advice he had heard around the theatres about this new medium of motion pictures, and how a guy with his stage experience would probably have no trouble getting a job either in front of or behind a camera. Chaney used what little money he had left to get to Universal Studios, located in an area of somewhat rugged, open land over the Cahuenga Pass—then just a rough dirt road—from Hollywood. It wouldn't take long for this burgeoning brainchild of New York entrepreneur Carl Laemmle to become the size of a small city and, appropriately enough, the location became known as "Universal City" in 1915.

At Universal, Chaney quickly progressed from a horse riding extra in Westerns to a versatile character actor often cast as the "heavy." The transition from stage to screen wasn't an especially easy one at first, and Chaney had his share of butterflies when it came time to stand in front of a motion picture camera: "I can't tell you the peculiar sensation which came over me as I stood for the first time opposite the camera to have the test made. The only way I could describe the sensation of breaking into the movies would be like dropping straight down in an elevator."[20]

Chaney had the intelligence to recognize the enormous potential of motion pictures, and lost no time in developing and honing his skills as a make-up artist and all-purpose actor. He would often surprise the powers-that-be by sporting outlandish disguises even when his job only called for him to shift scenery.[21] Chaney's single-minded, blisteringly intense focus on perfecting his craft, while directly contributing to his professional success, overshadowed every other aspect of his life. Nothing else seemed to matter to him until that day in early 1915 when he passed by a place called Jahnke's Tavern on the way home to his modest apartment on North Grand Avenue. Chaney noticed the tavern's sign board that advertised a singer named Hazel Hastings would be featured that evening. Hazel had once been described as being a "sweet, gentle little thing with a small sweet voice and tiny hands that fluttered like butterflies."[22] How could he ever forget the dark haired, petite (Hazel was a mere 4'10" tall), part-Italian girl who had been so kind to him during the days when she had worked as a chorus girl in the same Kolb & Dill company where Lon had his last stage job. At that time, they were both caught up in their own personal domestic tragedies and could do no more than exchange a few pleasant words. Chaney decided to go to Jahnke's that evening. After the show, Hazel agreed to join him at his table for a drink to talk about old times and do a little catching up. The connection between the two was immediate and passionate. Somehow they just knew they were meant to be together, and their conversations soon turned toward talk of marriage. By the summer of 1915, Lon had already proposed to Hazel, but she wasn't quite as eager to jump back into matrimony, especially with an actor. She'd had her fill of the crazy life of a performer and the constant traveling. She wanted a stable home, a family, and a regular husband who would be home every night for dinner. After all the hardship he'd endured over the years, Chaney dreamt of this kind of life, too. He wanted a wife who would be content to stay home, efficiently run his household, and provide the sort of personal support his soul longed for. It was also important to him that Creighton would finally have a good mother, and he yearned for the day his son could come live with him full time and never again have to be "farmed out." The marriage took place on November 26, 1915 in Santa Ana, and Hazel, Lon, and Creighton settled into their first home on Hudson Avenue in Los Angeles.[23]

On the surface, Hazel and Lon's story seems just too good to be true. They had each found in the other that missing part that was needed to complete them. The relationship was built on a deep understanding and trust that would be the basis for their genuine friendship and love. The two certainly had their differences, but any snag in the fabric of their lives was quickly smoothed over and forgotten. Hazel loved her new role as wife and step-mother to Lon's nine-year-old son, and Chaney now had the comfort and support he needed to give his full attention to furthering his career in motion pictures. With Hazel's keen intuition and business savvy, Lon was able to make more money and save more than he ever dreamed possible just a few short years before. His confidence increased dramatically and this new attitude enabled him to imbue his supporting performances with so much raw power that he often stole the picture away from the principal players. Hazel had a way of giving her husband a much-needed psychological push in the right direction, though it often took her own brand of filibustering to get her point across. Her perseverance was rewarded with Chaney's ever-increasing success.

Chaney's career quickly moved to the forefront in 1919 when he was given the role of a con-man who pretended to be a paralyzed beggar known as "The Frog" in director George Loane Tucker's production of *The Miracle Man*. This was the first time Chaney was required to not only alter his facial features, but his entire body to achieve the desired characterization.[24] Chaney was able to twist and bend his wiry dancer's physique into that of a paralytic cripple. Audiences were stunned, horrified, and delighted by Chaney's character's amazing "trick" of winding and unwinding his limbs at will. Many people believed Chaney had to be a contortionist to have accomplished such a feat, but the key was to be found in his expert acting ability and flexible joints. Even with his great skill, Chaney reportedly suffered a lasting, painful injury to his shoulder from popping it out during his performance in *The Miracle Man*. Incredibly, this injury only seemed to inspire Chaney to further test his physical and psychological limits to achieve the sort of characterizations no one had ever attempted before. He could put up with the pain if it meant achieving his goal to be the best at whatever he set his mind to.[25]

Chaney's genius for character work was in his uncanny facility for pantomime and the ability to see the shades of grey where other actors could only find the more obvious black and white. No character was all bad or all good in Chaney's book, and he sought to uncover the subtle nuances of even the most hardened criminal or deviant type. In a strange paradox of the human condition, it is ironic then that Chaney was never able to understand or sympathize with Cleva in any way. Her memory would always be veiled in total blackness.

Chaney's gift for complex characterizations and physical transformation raised itself to a new level in 1920 when he would be asked to play the legless character "Blizzard" from Governeur Morris' controversial 1913 novel, *The Penalty*. Determined to pull off the illusion of being a double amputee without the use of any photographic trickery, Chaney designed and built a leather harness that would strap his legs behind his back and "buckets" for his knees to fit in. He would walk on his knees with the aid of shortened crutches, just the way the artist Howard Chandler Christy had depicted the character in his illustrations for Morris' novel. Help was required to fit the harness on Chaney's body, tighten the straps, put on the buckets, and aid the actor in donning the rest of his costume. It was a *tour de force* performance, and the most painful and physically punishing that Chaney had yet experienced. Though some of the reports of Chaney's suffering were exaggerated for effect, he did disregard his doctor's warnings and kept his legs tightly bound much longer than was prudent. The result was pain so severe Chaney would collapse to the floor of the set while aides would rush over to loosen the harness and massage his legs to get the blood flowing again.[26] Chaney's desire to make the most of his opportunity to carry such an important picture caused him to recklessly disregard his own safety and well-being. He would suffer chronic back and neck pain for the rest of his life. For better or for worse, the pain Chaney inflicted on himself seemed to give him the edge he needed to focus all of his energy and concentration with razor-sharp precision on the characterization he envisioned for the undeniably evil, yet strangely sensitive and virile, "Blizzard." It would prove to be one of the most powerful performances of his career.

Chaney's success with *The Penalty* proved to be something of a double-edged sword in many ways. Audiences now wanted to see the actor in even more weird and grotesque parts, and the newspapers were referring to Chaney as a "delineator of cripples."[27] He could fight this attempt at typecasting, or use it to further climb the ladder to success. After portraying a variety of characters with mixed results, Chaney would once again return to the unusual roles that brought him the greatest acclaim, and also provided the best training ground for developing his ideas for new make-up techniques that would elevate the craft to a recognized art form. Before Chaney, individual actors were mainly responsible for their own make-up—there were no official make-up artists. Chaney's pioneering work in the field of motion picture make-up changed all of that, and laid the foundation for studios to later create entire make-up departments and hire professional artists.[28]

The Hunchback of Notre Dame by Victor Hugo held a special place in Chaney's heart for many reasons. The obvious one would be the extreme challenge it presented for recreating on screen the hideously deformed visage of the unfortunate hunchback, Quasimodo. On a deeper level, the character of Quasimodo represented all of the downtrodden, misunderstood, and physically imperfect people in the world that Chaney had an inherent desire to champion in his own way. Portraying this pitiful character in an impassioned and empathetic way would show the public that even the most repellant creature can have a beautiful soul. Chaney learned at a young age to be more tolerant of the handicapped and less fortunate in our society due to his parent's inability to hear or speak. Frank and Emma Chaney were in every respect hardworking and loving parents, who adored their four children (all of whom had normal hearing).[29] Still, there are people who can be very cruel to those who are considered to be outside the norm in one way or another, and Chaney had to deal with a lot of harsh comments and ignorance growing up. *The Hunchback of Notre Dame* would be his way of bringing his particular world-view to the public, though in a way that could be concealed within the guise of entertainment.

Jeske must have been overwhelmed by Chaney's offer to work for him, and wasted no time accepting the job and resigning from the auto repair shop. Mansey probably would have liked the job working for Chaney himself, but he was content to prove his worth as a mechanic and plan for the day when he could take over operating the garage. The three men would remain fast friends throughout the years to come.

For Jeske, this new position was the big break he was hoping for ever since he came to Los Angeles. Back in his room at the old boarding house, he excitedly wrote a letter to his brother Gus back in Scranton all about meeting Lon Chaney and being offered his important new job. Gus was the only family member that Jeske really felt a bond with, and they corresponded on an infrequent but steady basis. Gus' life revolved around the bakery and Julius' family (which had grown to include nine children), and he had very little of his own to brag about. Deep down, Jeske had a need to feel important, even if he didn't have the background and education required to rise above the menial jobs he usually had to take. A chauffeur could wear a nice uniform and at least look like he was "somebody," but there was something else that Chaney only hinted at that caught Jeske's attention; something about other work that needed to be done that had to be kept strictly on the q.t. Jeske, though no longer a kid at age 33, had that youthful restless quality in his nature that rebelled at too much predictability in his daily life. The everyday grind of a job, the everyday *sameness*, eventually bored Jeske to tears, and he longed to move on to new and more exciting ground. Something told him that this new job with Chaney was going to offer him the variety, stimulation, and prestige he craved. What he didn't realize just yet, and couldn't have foreseen at this early date, was that this new position would also bring the elements of true friendship, love, and family that had been sorely missed from his solitary life for so long.

Chaney's plan to infiltrate Jeske into his studio dressing room with as little fanfare as possible was a simple one. Journalist Adela Rogers St. Johns—a true pioneer in her own right—described a typical working day: "At 5 o'clock, just as the cold dawn was breaking over the studio, the gateman on duty would see the familiar roadster drive up, with John Jeske, silent and impenetrable, at the wheel, and Chaney, as silent, beside him. The gates would swing back upon the empty silence of the tremendous plant. Chaney would park his car in the most select spot—it always gave him a secret glee to put it in exactly the spot where the great executives could most conveniently descend to go up to their offices—and . . . Chaney and Jeske would enter the dressing room." St. Johns would go on to note that "No one could casually drop into Lon's dressing room . . . It was a holy of holies, a sanctum, a magician's cell . . . it was inviolate." But, as the astutely perceptive lady would record, "John Jeske was always in Lon's dressing room." Her claim may be a somewhat exaggerated one, but it is undeniable that Jeske soon became so much a part of Chaney's daily routine, and seen with the actor on the set and off, it was said that Jeske was like Lon Chaney's "shadow"—even his "second-self." St. Johns had been one of the reporters allowed into Chaney's dressing room when he was being fitted with his costume for the role of Quasimodo, and she saw Jeske—whom she described as being Chaney's dresser—assisting him.[30]

Chaney had found in Jeske not only a willing and malleable assistant, but a genial companion with whom he could "shoot the breeze" and help to fill the moments while they labored over his make-up and costume. He also enjoyed watching Jeske—carefully observing the way his face and body moved. Chaney's self-imposed isolation from the mainstream of Hollywood was a necessary safeguard for his privacy and sanity, but the side effect was a nagging loneliness and longing to share himself with someone.[31] Jeske had a natural charm, easy, warm smile and a quick wit, as well as a love of the outdoors and sports that proved a winning combination with Chaney. Jeske was much more fun loving and frivolous, though—qualities which strangely fascinated his rather conservative boss. Even more important, Chaney had found someone who knew the value of loyalty and friendship—the sort of things Chaney held dear to his heart. Jeske, on the other hand, had found in Chaney the noble man with high moral and ethical standards— a man of great importance—that he had idealized since his was a little boy. He was eager to prove his worth to Chaney by being "impenetrable" and the very model of discretion in all things. Deep down, his life needed the structure and order that would come from being in a subordinate—but very important—position as Chaney's assistant. Jeske was capable of giving himself completely to the task and taking whatever obligations he met with in stride. In time, he would learn a good many of Chaney's professional and personal secrets and yet he managed to bury them so deeply that no one could ever pry them loose from his memory.

Chaney could not have found a better man for the job.

Chapter 2:

LON CHANEY'S "FAITHFUL SERVANT" AND HIS SECRETS

Who exactly *was* Lon Chaney?

His legacy as an actor has been written about and analyzed for many years. His surviving body of work remains a testament to his remarkable genius, and critics and biographers have taken each film apart to find that missing piece of the puzzle that mystifies fans to the present day. With the large volume of written material and documentaries available on the subject, one wonders if anything new can really be discovered that would finally shed some light on Lon Chaney, the man. The focus of this chapter, therefore, will be on the human being behind the legend and his trusted friend who was almost obliterated from history.

At the end of 1924, John Jeske was officially Lon Chaney's make-up assistant, dresser, and whatever else the Boss needed. Jeske was also Chaney's stand-in, sparing the actor those long hours under the hot lights while the technicians readied the set and checked the lighting.[1] Jeske's height, weight, and coloring were nearly identical to Chaney's, so he made a good fit. Jeske was flexible, intelligent, and most importantly of all, discreet. Chaney had no fear of Jeske running to the newspapers with all the intimate details of the actor's personal life and make-up secrets. As far as anyone knew, Jeske was Chaney's chauffeur and personal assistant to Mrs. Chaney. He drove Hazel to the market and back, took care of their beloved dog, Sandy, sent out their Christmas cards, and often handled their other personal correspondence as well. Jeske was becoming indispensable to Chaney and more than just an employee. Chaney confided his innermost thoughts to Jeske while the two men labored together in the studio dressing room and when the work day was done, would often play cards with him and a few other trusted friends in the evening. Once or twice a week, Jeske may have found himself invited to join Chaney at one of his favorite pastimes—a boxing match. As Adele Rogers St. Johns had noted; Jeske was becoming Chaney's "second self," though by necessity, always hidden in the shadows.

The reason John Jeske has been excised from most biographies of Lon Chaney is something of a mystery. When Jeske is mentioned, the information is all too brief and many times inaccurate. Still, the bits and pieces planted within the story of Lon Chaney's career do give the thoughtful reader enough to pause and wonder; "Who was this John Jeske, and what was his real connection to Lon Chaney?" The truth is both poignant and inspirational and, most significantly of all, needs to be told in order to bring Jeske's contribution back into the light once more.

Jeske's work with Chaney on *The Hunchback of Notre Dame* led to his even more direct involvement with Chaney's next major make-up challenge: The role of Eric in Universal's version of Gaston Leroux's *The Phantom of the Opera.* With his newfound success with Chaney, Jeske was able to afford a new apartment on Maple Street, which was an improvement over his former downtown apartment. His social life was limited to the Chaneys at this point. Jeske remained at the ready at all times of day and night to be of assistance as needed. Jeske did enjoy a good cigar, though, and made friends with the clerks at the local cigar shop. His sense of loyalty to Chaney kept his employer out of any casual conversation he may have had with those he met in the shops or at the café. Jeske was friendly and easy to talk to, but he made sure no one ever got close to him.

Lon Chaney was a rare actor who never let his ego get in the way of his craft. He saw the work he did within the motion picture industry as a job. It was a job he enjoyed and took pride in, but a job all the same. He greatest wish was to go to the studio in the morning, put in his eight or so hours, and then go home to his personal life and family. Even in a "regular" job, this is no easy feat. People want you to socialize after hours, tell them all about your life and your innermost secrets, and generally hobnob with the "gang." Anyone who seems to deviate from the "norm" and appears over protective of their privacy, gets the stigma of being unfriendly, uncooperative, and somehow weird. Chaney's desire to shield his personal life—to actually have a full personal life—led to the many wild and mostly untrue stories about his deviant, anti-social behavior and overall dour personality. Yes, it's true that some of Chaney's desire for mystery was a very savvy marketing ploy to make people even more interested to find out who he was and what he was all about. Unfortunately, this method of generating publicity backfired and cast a heavy veil over Chaney's off-screen character. There are enough quotes from Chaney to make one believe this is exactly what he wanted, and he was adamantly against the idea of anyone trying to write his biography. There were secrets in Chaney's past—his first wife, for one—and secrets from his present life—like his heavy reliance on John Jeske—that were obvious reasons behind Chaney's wish to not have his story told.

Chaney, the artist, was humble enough to know that he needed help at times to realize his most fantastic make-up ideas. He had used a dentist to design and produce the false teeth he wore as Quasimodo[2] and worked with other make-up technicians at Universal to help create the plaster "hump" and rubber shirt he wore in the film. There were Chaney films that were not as challenging in terms of make-up. In *He Who Gets Slapped* (MGM: 1924), for example, he used traditional clown make-up. He would later create his own look when he played a circus clown again in *Laugh, Clown, Laugh* (MGM: 1928); this vehicle provided Chaney an opportunity to develop his acting talent. Victor Seastrom, who directed *He Who Gets Slapped*, said of the star: "I don't believe Chaney's wonderful ability as an actor has ever been really appreciated."[3] Though physically demanding, these films provided a welcome break from the grueling, almost masochistic discipline Chaney put himself through to achieve his greatest characterization to date in *The Hunchback of Notre Dame*. There are stories of Chaney passing out on the set from the heat and strain and spending time in the hospital for exhaustion. When journalist Adela Rogers St. Johns visited the set and saw what she described as Chaney's "self-torture," she claims to have been physically sickened by the spectacle, and told Chaney of her misgivings. She claims he looked at her with wild eyes and snapped, "This is truth, not acting. I'm not playing a hunchback with a bundle of straw on my back. I *am* a hunchback. I know how it feels. I've only got one eye with that make-up, to show them the torments of that poor deformed soul and body. Well, that eye will show it because I feel it. I'll show 'em. I can do it."[4]

Chaney was able to do it, and do it better than anyone else ever could, but at what cost? St. Johns wrote years later that Chaney was never quite the same again after he realized his dream to bring Quasimodo to the screen. That certain "spark" she had noticed in the eyes of the young actor she met back in 1916 was gone after 1924, that he wasn't the "vital, dynamic person" she had known.[5] What it was replaced with was not as yet quite defined, but resembled more a look of fatigue and a sort of resignation that had never been a part of Chaney before.

Production began on Universal's *The Phantom of the Opera* in October of 1924. Not only would this film give Chaney the opportunity to create his most startling, bone-chilling characterization yet, but also give him one more chance to get back at the studio that once said he'd never be worth more than $100 per week.[6] His salary was now a whopping $2,000 per week and he would have complete creative freedom over his make-up work, though the latter perk was not achieved without some heated back-and-forth discussion between Chaney's manager and Universal.[7] The horribly disfigured and tortured soul that was Eric, the opera "phantom," was perfect for Chaney's sensibilities. Here was another misunderstood pariah who Chaney could show as being not a monster, but simply a tormented soul who longs to be accepted and loved. That theme reverberates throughout nearly all of Chaney's film roles. As he told journalist Lee Shippey: "I like to show that there's good in the most loathsome creature alive if the right person or the right circumstances brings it out. I like the underdog in every fight—not if he's quitting like a cur, but if he's giving all he's got. I like prize fights, and my sympathies are always with the fellow who's getting licked."[8]

To begin work on his characterization, Chaney went back to the source—Gaston Leroux's original novel—and found illustrations that hinted at the extent of the disfigurement of Eric's face and his severely emaciated appearance. He based his initial designs for the make-up on these ideas and sought a way to translate them to film. As always, Chaney's way was not the easy way, and his design included wires, twisted, gnarled dentures to alter the shape of his mouth, and other physically painful devices. Cameraman Charles Van Enger recalled in an interview given in 1974 that "[Chaney] had two wires under his nose that pulled—that went up the bridge of the nose, were taped down with makeup to hide them and then up under his bald wig where they were tied, like and Indian headband, with a thin leather strap. Some days that thing would bleed like hell. This thing with the nose up like that all the time and these rubber stoppers shoved in his nostrils; ears taped back and those wires in his mouth to hold the gums back—I don't know how he stood the pain. But he did and we never had to stop shooting any of his scenes."[9]

Jeske had a knack with anything mechanical and was adept at working with wire and making harnesses, or whatever was required. Whether it was Jeske who assembled the nose piece with wires hooked to a headband, or Jack Pierce, as claimed by MGM studio organist Chauncey Haines[10], it was no secret on the set that Chaney had helpers, and this fact was even revealed in newspaper articles written about his work.[11] The *ideas* were Chaney's, but he needed help with the more technical aspects of the design to make them real. The bits and pieces alone would mean nothing if they were not assembled with Chaney's artistic genius and craftsmanship. MGM studio manager J.J. Cohn knew of Jeske's more practical talents and said, "I used to borrow [Jeske] from time to time when we had a problem with our trucks on the back lot."[12]

The Phantom of the Opera was released on September 6, 1925, in New York. When the film premiered in Los Angeles, Mr. and Mrs. Lon Chaney made a rare appearance. Missing from the crowd was Creighton Chaney, now a young man of nineteen. Chaney did his best to provide his son with a stable home and a strong work ethic, but the emotionally scarred boy needed more encouragement and love than his old-school father felt it was appropriate to give. Creighton had been expelled from high school for fighting after being bullied unmercifully for months. Not only did he knock out the main bully who made his life miserable, he also methodically made a list and beat up every single boy who had ever hurt him.

Though personally satisfying, this act of revenge only resulted in Creighton's expulsion. His father was upset at the news, yet at the same time proud that his son had finally stood up for himself. Lon enrolled Creighton at the Disabled American Veteran's Institute which was designed to rehabilitate war veterans and teach them a trade: "Father was still hipped on my becoming a bank teller, so I entered an army rehabilitation school open to the public. I did the one-and-a half-year course in six months and came out supposedly able to handle business details."[13] As Chaney would later comment to Adela Rogers St. Johns about Creighton's decision not to attend college: "The Chaneys don't run to that sort of thing. He'd better go to work and make a man out of himself."[14] After graduating from the Institute, Creighton took his father's advice and became an apprentice at a water heating company owned by Ralph L. Hinckley.

There are many rumors and stories about why Creighton did not attend the premiere of *Phantom*—an act some see as a deliberate slap in his father's face—but few can be substantiated at this late date. Around this time, Creighton is said to have been furious when he discovered his real mother was alive and well and living only a short distance away in Pasadena.[15] Cleva had remarried a farmer by the name of Bush and had a daughter, Stella. Chaney had worked hard to create the illusion that Cleva had died many years ago and made no effort to correct the general misconception that Hazel was Creighton's mother.[16] Chaney undoubtedly made it difficult for a full-fledged reunion between Creighton and his real mother, but it was no longer possible for Lon to hide the truth and his son resented the years of deception. Shortly before the *Phantom* premiere, he took Hazel and Creighton on a three-week vacation to his favorite getaway spot high in the Sierra Nevada Mountains to the little town of Big Pine. They would need to leave their car in nearby Bishop and go the rest of the way by horseback.[17] This was a good time for Chaney to get away from all the distractions of Hollywood and have the time to talk to his son—man to man. The two would eventually reconcile, but there was a distance between them that could never quite be bridged.

Hazel Chaney was something of a wiz in the area of investments, and her investment of choice was Hollywood real estate. She often used Jeske to scout out new properties, to take care of small details with the real estate agents, and to run documents back and forth to the Courthouse. Chaney trusted his wife implicitly with his money and knew she had the head for practical dollars and cents business he lacked. The Chaneys had a great balance in their marriage that proved successful for both their personal and financial well-being. There are those who said Chaney would sometimes chafe at the way Hazel would keep them on such a tight budget that his own money was rationed to him[18], but for the most part he was proud of his wife's business acumen. By allowing Hazel the freedom to manage the money and their home, Chaney had the freedom to concentrate on his work without worrying about how the bills will get paid and if there would be money in the bank for tomorrow. Chaney's early history of poverty made him anxious about the future and determined to stockpile as much money as he could to prevent any chance of being in the street in his old age. For all his outward confidence, Chaney was insecure about his place in Hollywood and felt the rug could be pulled out from under him at any moment, so he'd better have a back-up plan. Chaney was noted for often giving advice to younger actors and actresses about thinking of the future: "Save your money. Take care of your health. Why, I'll be able to work when I'm a hundred. I've taken care of myself. I'll never know want. Always remember you've got to think about the future. You can't live just for today."[19]

As the year 1926 began, Chaney was thinking about the future more than ever. It is true that Chaney took care of his health, exercised as often as he could at the Hollywood Athletic Club, and ate well thanks to Hazel. What Chaney didn't realize was how the years of chain-smoking were starting to take their toll on him no matter how hard he tried to fight off the effects. Chaney began to notice his energy level wasn't as high as it used to be—he couldn't catch his breath once in a while—things that had previously seemed physically easy for him were now more difficult. He kept this hidden for now, determined he could single-handedly beat whatever it was that plagued him, and went on with his business as usual. At the studio, he would confide in Jeske about his hopes and dreams and shared his fears with him as well. Adela Rogers St. Johns was present one day in Chaney's dressing room when he read to Jeske a verse from the Bible his mother had loved.[20] Chaney had been raised a Christian and lived his life by the principles of his faith, though he relied heavily on his own will power to get him through: "Everything I am I made myself. Everything I've got I got for myself."[21] Hazel was a strong Christian, too, and had been raised as a Catholic, though she was not active in her church since marrying outside her faith.

The Chaneys had moved to a small but picturesque English Tudor-style home located at 604 Linden Drive, in what was even then the posh neighborhood of Beverly Hills. The couple had plans for a bigger and better home of their own to be built, so this new residence was only a rental. It had big picture windows and a large fireplace in the living room that made the cozy surroundings a warm and welcome place for the Chaneys to entertain their close circle of friends. Chaney shunned the Hollywood lifestyle and chose his friends carefully from the people who had been with him from the early days of his career: Clinton and Florence (Flo) Lyle; Fay Parkes (who had taken care of little Creighton during Chaney's vaudeville days) and her lawyer husband Phil Epstein; actor M.K. Wilson and his wife; comic-actor Eddie Gribbon, businessman William Dunphy and his wife Mabel; and, of course, there was John Jeske. Chaney's studio pals, musicians Sam and Jack Feinberg, were sometimes guests in the Chaney home. Though this was still during the Prohibition, alcohol flowed freely and there was no shortage of good beer and wine, or whatever else was required. Creighton remembered many years later how his father liked to have a cocktail before dinner, and when he was old enough, his father made one for him, too.[22]

At the tender age of twenty, Creighton Chaney married the boss's daughter—a beautiful young lady named Dorothy—on April 25, 1926. Papa Hinckley made sure the young man was worthy of his daughter by putting him through various trials and tribulations to test his mettle.[23] He must have been impressed enough to give his blessing to the nuptials. Creighton's parents were equally happy with the turn of events, and Chaney felt relieved that his troubled boy was finally on the right path (or so it seemed).

Jeske found himself to be a part of the Chaney's lives, yet never quite a full participant. He was there with them to celebrate the good times and lend a sympathetic ear during the times of trouble. Jeske was always relegated to the fringes of the Chaney's world, even though he was frequently observed with Chaney and working on his behalf and that of Mrs. Chaney. This close association with Chaney caused a rift between Jeske and Creighton that was simmering on the back burner for now, but would later come to a full boil when triggered by the chaotic events to come in the near future. Even though Chaney himself was extremely tolerant of different ethnic groups and cultures, his son seemed to have embraced the dislike of "foreigners"—especially those of German descent like Jeske—that was prevalent in this post-World War I environment.[24]

Production began in early February of 1927 on a film that would was released with the enigmatic title: *The Unknown*. The director was one very familiar to Chaney—Tod Browning. They had completed two pictures together in 1926 (*The Blackbird* and *Road to Mandalay*), which would make *The Unknown* their seventh collaboration to date. The relationship between Browning and Chaney has been the source of a great deal of speculation and theories, but the two men made sure if there was a deeper level to their association it would forever be their secret. On the surface, Browning was not the best director in Hollywood, had a serious drinking problem, and was mainly liked by the studios for bringing his films in under budget and in record time. The scripts were often penned by Browning himself and he frequently reused plot ideas and characters so that his films seem to all have a sameness that can cause the viewing public to grow very weary of them in record time as well. What Browning did add to the mix was a taste for the bizarre and a fondness for human oddities of all kinds. Why a top actor like Chaney would want to work with Browning is the real mystery. It is a documented fact that Chaney's non-Browning directed films earned more money than his work with Browning.[25] And yet, Browning allowed Chaney the creative freedom he required to design and implement whatever make-up and devices he wanted to in order to realize the characterization he had in mind for a particular role. Browning gave him free reign to develop the characters and bring them to the screen. His direction of Chaney was minimal, and that is exactly the way Chaney liked it. What Chaney didn't like was Tod Browning as a human being. Browning was an alcoholic and an adulterer, traits that surely offended Chaney's sense of morality and fair play. There was no close friendship between the two men. Chaney used Browning for his own purposes and kept the relationship strictly business at all times. Adela Rogers St. Johns was on the set one day when she observed one of the many disagreements between Browning and Chaney: "They fought like a couple [of] sea lions. They yelled and cussed each other out plenty. But just let anyone else interfere. Let any executive or writer attempt to take advantage of the apparent friction. They soon found out it was a very private fight. Tod and Lon instantly ganged up on the intruder, who decided that he would be better occupied elsewhere."

Browning acknowledged the frequent arguments with Chaney, but said when it came time for the camera to roll, "he was a good soldier."[26]

The "good soldier" was becoming increasingly fatigued on the set. The drain on Chaney's physical energy continued to plague the actor no matter what he tried to do. Extra rest, more protein in his diet (his doctors were treating him for anemia, thinking it was an iron deficiency that caused his weakness), and other health measures were not working. It has been suggested that Chaney's decline in health may have been the main reason he made the generally inferior films with Tod Browning instead of taking on more challenging projects with more demanding and respected directors. Chaney must have had an understanding with Browning and even with all of Browning's other troubles, Chaney knew he was someone who would not betray the true nature of his health to anyone. Even so, it was apparent to Chaney's co-stars that something wasn't quite right. Joan Crawford, who played "Nanon" in *The Unknown*, remembered that Chaney did have help with his make-up for this film: "Every day he would arrive at the set with his driver who would get things ready for his shoot. Often, during the day, the assistant would run out to the drug store for make-up or the market on Washington for lunch. I believe [Jeske] had something to do with the large switches that were supposed to hold back the horses in the final scene. This was the only time that I saw someone double for Mr. Chaney. I believe he wasn't feeling too well at the time. His assistant would double for him in the knife throwing scene, but I don't remember much else, like if it made it to the screen."[27]

St. Johns was even more to the point about the situation: "Lon relied on his man Jeske more and more from 1927–1929. You don't get what Lon had in a few months and then just die from it. I would visit [Chaney] on the set and although I never saw his son . . . I did see Jeske with towel and water bottle, like a fighter's helper, always there on the ready. They even looked alike, you know. . . ."[28]

The costume Chaney had to wear in *The Unknown* to simulate an armless man (carnival performer "Alonzo the Armless") consisted of a girdle type of garment worn under his loosely fitting shirt that would conceal his arms by tightly lacing them up to his sides with his hands folded one on top the other inside his pants. It was impossible for Chaney to wipe his brow or touch-up his make-up between takes in this painful get-up, so it stands to reason he had to have help. As St. Johns observed: "To conceal his arms he wore a strait-jacket [sic] so tight that it broke the veins in his legs by the pressure of the blood pumping down from the strapped-up part of his body. Chaney put it on day after day and worked for hours. Sweat poured down his face and he had to have John Jeske always at hand to help renew his grease paint. At night, when he removed the jacket, his arms and back were a mass of black-and-blue bruises."[29]

Production of *The Unknown* wrapped up around March 18th, and Chaney was already making plans to get out of town for a much-needed rest. Toward the end of the month, Chaney and Hazel headed north—first to San Francisco to visit with Hazel's family and mutual friends and then the couple would drive up the coast to Oregon. While in San Francisco, Chaney took the opportunity to do some research for his next characterization in the film *Mockery*, to be directed by Danish director Benjamin Christensen. In this dark tale filled with disturbing subliminal psychology set during the Russian Revolution, Chaney was to play a poor, ignorant peasant caught between the two forces at play. "Sergei" was a slow moving, slow thinking beast with a child-like quality and, as always, a good heart. Chaney described his process for developing his characterization to a journalist: "To learn more about the Russian peasant, I visited a little film theatre in San Francisco, watching for a peasant type among the audience that would fit in with the character I was to play. Finally, I came across the man I wanted and I watched him closely. I first noted that there was in this man a sort of obstruction between perception and reaction. For instance, a thing had to sink in before the face disclosed knowledge of it, as though the message to the brain had been slightly dulled in transit. The character of Sergei, therefore, had to be not a little dumb, at least in so far as his physical expressions went. This denseness was reflected also by his gait; a careless shuffle; by his slouchy carriage, his loosely swinging arms and his general air of lethargy and inefficiency."[30]

The Chaneys were in Portland, Oregon, on the 8th or the 9th of the month when they received an urgent message from Los Angeles that Lon's father, Frank Chaney, had suffered a stroke and was not expected to recover. They rushed home as fast as they could and Lon was able to just make it to his father's bedside at the Methodist Hospital before the elder Chaney passed away on April 11th. Lon was very close to his father and he was distraught over the loss. Frank Chaney was a very outgoing, likeable man who made many friends in the deaf-mute community in Los Angeles and belonged to several organizations that catered to the deaf. He had married a deaf-mute lady named Cora he had met at one of the many functions he loved to attend and the two were very happy together. Chaney got along well with Cora, and was undoubtedly pleased to see his father enjoying his new life in Southern California. Frank Chaney's funeral was held at the chapel of the Bressee Brothers funeral home on South Figueroa Street. The Chaney children were there: Lon, John, George, and Carrie, as well as their families. The funeral was meant to be a private family affair, but Frank's many deaf friends wanted to pay their respects too and made their way inside the chapel. The service was conducted in sign-language amid the many beautiful floral pieces sent by friends and colleagues of Franks' actor-son Lon.[31] Frank was interred at the Forest Lawn Mausoleum in an unmarked crypt, as per his request.

Chaney had a little time in-between pictures to get some much-needed rest at home with his family. Jeske took the opportunity to take care of something he had wanted to do for years. On April

20th, Jeske went down to the courthouse and filed a Petition for Naturalization to complete the process he had begun in 1920 to become a full U.S. citizen. The affidavit also contains Jeske's request to legally change his name from "John Friedrich Jeske" to "John Fred Jeske." The witnesses were his acquaintances from the nearby cigar store, F. C. and George Overton. It was all a part of his desire to fully embrace his new country and put his troubled past behind him once and for all. Jeske had lost touch with most of his family, except for the occasional letters to his big brother, Gus, and wanted no part of the painful legacy his family represented to him. He had a new family now—Lon and Hazel Chaney—and a purpose in his life that gave him the stability he needed. Jeske had recently moved to a new apartment on Hollywood Boulevard just across the street from Grauman's Chinese Theatre. Like Jeske's other homes, this apartment would only contain him for a short while. The neighborhood was bustling with activity night and day, though not nearly as congested as in modern times.

Before beginning work on his next film, Chaney left town in early May for a short trip to the nearby Angeles National Forest to stay a few days at the relaxing Valley Ford Lodge. It always helped to relieve his mind to take time to get away from it all and do some fly fishing. Fishing was one of Chaney's greatest passions in life and he would talk anyone's ear off on the subject if they gave him half a chance. Jeske enjoyed the outdoors and the tranquility of the mountains almost as much as Chaney did, and often accompanied his boss on his frequent camping trips. Hazel usually came with them, but not always. There is very little of Hazel's innermost thoughts left to study, but if journalist Adela Rogers St. Johns can be believed, Hazel really didn't like roughing it in the mountains or fishing. It was something she did out of her deep love for her husband: "Her thought was always to please him. There wasn't anything she hated as much as outdoor life. Horseback riding was torture to her. Camping filled her with horror. But, she went on horseback into the mountains and camped for weeks and Lon never dreamed that she didn't enjoy it as much as she did."[32]

After the filming of *Mockery* wrapped near the end of June, Tod Browning once again approached Chaney with another of his unusual script ideas. This new film would give Chaney a chance to play two characters: A respectable police detective and a hideous creature the detective uses as a device to lure the real criminal out into the open. The working title of the project was, *The Hypnotist*, from a story by Browning. Browning called upon his usual collaborator, Waldemar Young, to work out the screenplay. The film would eventually be released to the theatres as *London After Midnight*.[33] Chaney required very little make-up to create his Detective Burke of the Scotland Yard outside of a applying a bit of grey to his temples and the affectation of a monocle. The creature the detective creates is a "vampire" with sharp, pointed teeth, a hideous, perpetual grin and unblinking eyes who slinks about the mansion in a bizarre simian gait; he is dressed in a long black overcoat and a top hat made out of beaver skin. For Chaney, this was the character that would be a real challenge to bring to the screen in a believable fashion. Chaney made use of Jeske's mechanical skill to devise a way to add fabric bat wings to the overcoat worn by the vampire, and make special wire fittings to keep Chaney's eyes and mouth open. A. Arnold Gillespie, who along with Cedric Gibbons designed the set for *London After Midnight*, remembered Jeske as "a quiet fellow—looked like Chaney. [Jeske] came to me one day to deliver a note regarding the bat wings Chaney was going to wear in a scene. Lon was told because of studio insurance on him he couldn't do it—so they were wondering if I could come up with a special effect. Later I came over to the set and Chaney's assistant was helping him with his suit. The suit had wires in a bat wing-type web that would appear when he raised his arms. His assistant would pat him on the back when he found a weak spot and sew the seams together. Chaney stopped, took off the coat and I told him that it would require reworking the set to accomplish his flying bat man idea, so they dropped it and had the girl vampire fly. [Chaney's] helpers were there in the dressing room, especially after the industry switched from orthochromatic to panchromatic film. They would apply the appliances and make-up where he couldn't reach and touchups on locations, and one used to stand in for him."[34]

The nearly non-stop filming schedule and the loss of his father took a heavy toll on Chaney, physically and emotionally. Not long after completing his work on *London*, Chaney once again retreated to Big Pine in the Sierra Nevada Mountains where his favorite fishing spot was located up the hill from the Glacier Pack Train station. Jeske went with him this time and helped to navigate the big sedan along the rough roads from Los Angeles to the mountains. The trip was approximately 282 miles long, but in the days when highways were merely gravel roads, the journey could take up to seven hours. An article published in the *Los Angeles Times* described what the brave traveler had in store for them: "Wide gravel road, rough in places, is then traversed to Indian Wells, with good natural gravel road via Little Lake to Coso Junction. Wide graded highway, corduroyed and chucky for light cars, is then traversed to Lone Pine, with excellent natural gravel road for 5.5 miles, then chucky gravel road to Independence and excellent oiled gravel highway the remaining distance to Big Pine, except for 8.2 miles of eight-foot pavement and some short sections of gravel." It was a rough ride, but well worth it to Chaney and his fishing buddy.

The date was not been recorded, but it was around this time that Chaney arranged to have a special cabin built for his friend Jeske on the banks of Big Pine Creek toward the end of Glacier Lodge Road. The finished cabin was a very comfortable little getaway nestled between the large pine trees with two bedrooms, a small kitchen, a large main room, porch, and a full basement for storage.[35] Chaney probably used the cabin himself prior to having his beautiful stone cabin built in 1930. Before Jeske's cabin was built, Chaney would have camped out in a tent along the banks of Big Pine Creek. In addition to fishing, Chaney enjoyed "hunting"—only his prey was shot with a camera and not a gun. Photography was another of Chaney's passions and he enjoyed taking still photos and using his brand new 16mm movie camera at home and at the studio.[36] There is evidence that Chaney also tried his hand at creating his own films complete with title cards,[37] but unfortunately these, too, have been lost or destroyed.

As October came around and the mountain air began to chill dramatically, signaling the coming of a harsh winter, Chaney and Jeske returned to Los Angeles. Tod Browning once again had a new project for Chaney, only this time there would be no handicap or deformity in his characterization. This picture was to be a sort of formulaic tale of the underworld with Chaney as a two-bit gangster named Chuck Collins. There was also a subplot involving a romance between Chuck and his maul, Helen. *The Big City* is one of the few late-1920s MGM films that were somehow lost, so it is impossible to know for sure what the quality of this film really was. It was generally panned by the critics when it was released in March of 1928, but while it was in production, Chaney had the rare luxury of not having to spend hour upon hour in his dressing room before the cameras rolled. To pass the time between filming, Chaney enjoyed the company of his two musician buddies, Sam and Jack Feinberg. Adela Rogers St. Johns preserved this record of their friendship: "Perhaps no one knew Lon better than Jack and Sam [Feinberg]. In the long, long hours that he put in at the studio, they where his constant companions. They were his playmates and his relaxation. He liked to rough-house with them, cuss them, pull their ears, and knock them about. They had a game which all three loved: Jack and Sam would get out the violin and the old organ. Lon would stand beside them. Lon would name any song—going back mostly to the old musical shows. The boys would play it. If he named a tune they couldn't play, they lost . . . The loser had to buy lunch in the commissary."[38] Another pastime was tap-dancing, and Chaney could go for hours dancing to the Feinberg's music making up new routines as he went along. It was his way of keeping fit and an attempt to stave off the effects of the mysterious illness that sought to rob him of his vitality.

While Chaney played, Jeske would have been setting things up on the set, running errands, or even at the Chaney home with Hazel doing odd jobs and driving her to hair appointments and the market. Jeske didn't always do the driving, though. Chaney loved his vehicles and liked driving himself around town now and then. Unfortunately, his lead foot got the best of him one day in December of 1927 and he was pulled over by two County Motor Patrolmen for driving 32 miles per hour in a 20 mph zone. Chaney was also cited for failing to report a change of address and ordered to appear in court on the 21st of December or face being arrested and put in jail.[39]

This incident took place during production of one of Chaney's best films, *Laugh, Clown, Laugh*, directed by his friend, Herbert Brenon. Chaney played the tragic Italian clown Tito Beppi who, along with his partner, Simon, adopted a toddler who had been abandoned by the side of a river. The girl, later given the name "Simonetta," grows up to be a beautiful young lady and Tito falls hopelessly in love with her. It's a rather disturbing plot at times, but the subject matter lends itself well to Chaney's powerful talent as an actor in being able to portray the subtleties of emotion and project his heartbreak to the audience. For his clown make-up, Chaney took the opportunity to create his own design while in keeping with the traditions of the circus clown.

Loretta Young, who had her 15th birthday during production, co-starred with Chaney as Simonetta. Some years ago, she talked with author Philip Riley about working on *Laugh, Clown, Laugh* and remembered John Jeske: "Mr. Chaney had his assistant helping him with the wire that went from the top of the set rigging to the stage. I believe the assistant had invented the apparatus that attached to the head and the bottom of the rope, because every time something went wrong he went over there to fix it. [Jeske] even looked like Mr. Chaney, except he had a moustache." This wire Young spoke about was the death-defying stunt Tito performed in his act—the one that eventually gave him an opportunity to end his life in order to provide his young charge with a chance at her own happiness with the handsome and very wealthy Count Luigi Ravelli. No one has yet come forward to identify the stunt man who actually performed this feat on camera for the film, but one could easily speculate it was Jeske.

Hollywood was a fast-moving place filled with scores of young men and women who flocked to this "magic" piece of real estate to find fame and fortune. So many ended up destitute and disillusioned, and so many more felt they could not live a "normal" life once they had tasted the materialism and decadence of the "party" crowd. The late 1920s was a time of underground liquor and sexual experimentation on a level not seen again in this country until the mid-1960s. One young couple caught up in this whirlwind was Paul and Elaine Beuter. The Beuters were a prominent family in Los Angeles and Paul was an up and coming advertising executive. Grace Elaine Cadwallader was a poor farm girl from Wisconsin who came to California with her overbearing mother Gertrude after her father died. Gertrude found work at MGM

Studios in the set department as a draper and Elaine did a little stenography and other secretarial work for actor Richard Dix (Ernest Brimmer). In her spare time, Elaine worked on her own ideas for films and got her big break in 1927 writing the story and screenplay for a low-budget picture called *Pirates in the Sky* for Hurricane Films. The following year Elaine wrote the screenplay for the Peerless Pictures release, *Bitter Sweets*. Elaine used the pseudonym "Elaine Wilmont" for her writing so as not to embarrass her husband's more conservative family. All this was heady stuff to the ambitious young woman and she wanted more. Paul enjoyed the high life for a time—he even partied with William Randolph Hearst on his infamous yacht—but his career was more important. When he received an offer to work for the big manufacturing company MJB in San Francisco, he jumped at the chance. Elaine was furious, but dutifully followed her husband to their new home.

While at MGM Studios, Elaine and her mother kept their eyes open for any and all opportunities to better themselves. For reasons unknown, Jeske caught Elaine's attention and she made herself known to him whenever their paths crossed. She told him she was only 21 years old, when in actuality she was three years older. Jeske, now 37 years old, was a fine looking man, athletic, and somewhat exotic due to his foreign origins, so it is possible Elaine was smitten with him for those reasons. His personality was quick and friendly, and his worldliness could have been a welcome relief to the monotony of her ad exec husband. Then again, maybe it was Jeske's close association to one of the top actors of his day and all the potential wealth he could possess that was the deciding factor. Whatever happened at the studio during those days and months; a seed was planted that would soon take root and produce bitter fruit.

Jeske's petition to become a full U.S. citizen was accepted and filed on February 17, 1928. It was a happy time for Jeske and he was thankful for all that his new country had given him. The New Year was somewhat more subdued for Jeske's boss, Chaney. There were a couple of film roles that didn't require a great deal of make-up work, and the opportunity to write about his craft in an article published in the *Academy Digest* titled, "The Effects of Make-up Under Incandescent Lights."

It was around this same time that movie studios—MGM being the first—established their own full make-up departments. In June of 1928, make-up artists from all studios created their own organization with the help of cosmetic pioneer Max Factor. The organization was known as the "Make-up Artists Association" and the presiding officers were Perc Westmore, Mel Barnes, Charles Dudley, Max Feuerstein, and Bert Hadley. A shift in methodology was taking place that would separate the actor from his make-up in a very tangible way. Mel Barnes was quoted by a newspaper reporter as saying: "A production cannot exist without an actor, and the character actor cannot exist without the make-up artists. It is he [the make-up artist] who creates the character you see portrayed before you on the screen."[40] One can only wonder what Chaney's opinion of all this talk was. Obviously, Chaney was a character actor who relied on his own skill to design the make-up for his characterizations. It is true that he had help, but his helpers—Jeske included—did not supersede Chaney's genius in the art of motion picture make-up. It would not be long before make-up artists would unionize and prevent character actors—or any other actors, for that matter—from doing their own make-up, and so ended an era of individual pioneers in the field that allowed a talent like Chaney to excel.

By 1928 there was also a shift within the motion picture industry to start making talking pictures exclusively. *The Jazz Singer* was released in the U.S. in 1927 and audiences were crazy about this part-"talkie." Silent films would be made for another year or so, but by 1928, the proverbial handwriting was on the wall. Chaney was adamantly against the idea of talking pictures. "I won't make the damn noisy, squeaky things," Chaney said to his friend, journalist Adela Rogers St. Johns one day in 1929.[41] He held out a long time, too, but finally gave in to the lure of the big money offered by MGM in1930 to do a sound remake of his 1925 Tod Browning-directed silent film, *The Unholy Three*. Charlie Chaplin was the final hold-out to sound films and he managed to avoid making one until 1936. Chaney's reasons for not wanting to make sound films were partly professional—he was a master of pantomime and would need an entirely new approach to make sound films—but a large part of his objection to sound was the fact that the deaf community would no longer have this outlet for entertainment.

Chaney would release two more films in 1928: A straightforward character study of a middle-aged, police detective suffering from job burnout and unrequited love in *While the City Sleeps*; and another twisted, bitter, and heart-broken misfit in Tod Browning's *West of Zanzibar* (based on the sordid stage play, *Kongo*, by Charles de Vond and Kilbourn Gordon). In the latter film, Chaney portrays a man who had been paralyzed from the waist down and was limited to crawling on the floor or pulling himself up into a wheelchair in order to get around. The strain on Chaney's back must have been enormous and severely painful. After completing *The Unknown* the previous year, Chaney had confided to his friend, journalist Clarence Locan, "I can't play these crippled roles anymore. That trouble with my spine is worse every time I do one, and it's really beginning to worry me."[42] The pressure was building within Chaney, for he knew his time in front of the camera was short, yet he didn't want to let on to Hazel or his family that anything was wrong.

Chaney especially didn't want Hazel to know that he was in bad shape now that they were finally going to realize a dream they had had for many years to build a real Hollywood mansion to spend the rest of their days in. They had gone ahead with plans to hire noted architect Paul Revere Williams, who in 1921 became the first African-American architect to be certified west of the Mississippi,[43] to design and supervise the building of their home, which was to be located at 806 Whittier Drive in Beverly Hills. A newspaper article about the Chaney mansion described the finished home as being of the "Italian type with a golden colored tile roof and whitewashed brick exterior walls. To obtain an appearance of age, the bricks were selected from those of a sixty-five-year-old Los Angeles building that had recently been razed. A combination radio and phonograph that can be controlled from any principal room was built into the house, the loud speakers being concealed behind the wall canvas. The kitchen is entirely of tile. In the library, a section of the chestnut paneled walls slides back to reveal a buffet."[44]

1929 had arrived and by mid-year a lot of work still needed to be done to complete this fantastic structure. The Chaneys found themselves in a bind. The lease on the home on Linden Drive was up and they were forced to move their belongings out before their new home was finished. Jeske and mutual friend Louis Mansey helped move out some of the Chaney furniture and store it in a home the Mansey's owned on Laurel Avenue—just down the street from where Creighton and his family were living. A bedroom set and some miscellaneous tables and chairs were kept there until the Chaney's could retrieve the items to put in his new home.[45] Chaney was in no shape physically to be of much help and, in fact, required more help than ever from his trusted friend, Jeske. There is evidence to support the idea that Jeske had to help Chaney with some basic day-to-day tasks now, which would explain why the Chaneys and Jeske moved into a duplex located at 203 S. Mansfield. It is a comfortable little home located in a quiet suburb on a corner lot. The Chaneys had one side and Jeske occupied the other—available at any time of day or night. Chaney's personal situation was becoming more desperate now, and yet the desire to keep his failing health a secret was paramount in his mind. Even Creighton was kept from the truth, though it was obvious to him that his father was in serious trouble.[46]

In July of 1928, Chaney's first grandchild, Lon Ralph Chaney, had been born, and Chaney was overjoyed and eager to play the role of the proud grandfather: "I'm grandpop now. Guess I can spoil this one. Creighton'll have to look after him. I can have some fun." Chaney made toys for his little namesake out of clay and wood and played with baby Lon as much as his schedule would allow.[47] Another year had passed and it was time for Chaney to go back to work.

Chaney agreed to work with Tod Browning again on another tired, rehashed script taken from many of Browning's other films to be titled *Where East Is East.* The film is set in Indo-China with Chaney as "Tiger" Haynes, a wild animal trapper who lives alone with his half-Chinese daughter Toyo, played by twenty year-old Mexican actress Lupe Velez. Estelle Taylor (who was married to heavyweight boxing champion Jack Dempsey), played the part of Tiger's malevolent ex-wife, Madame de Silva, whose evil plans work to destroy the happiness of the daughter she abandoned at birth and in so doing destroy the ex-husband who sent her packing so many years ago. Velez had a reputation for being a little hard to handle, but she behaved herself with Chaney, who described her as a "great little actress."[48] The usually vivacious Taylor found herself playing a rather subdued role that called for more subtlety than she was used to. She felt totally wrong for the part of Madame de Silva and wanted out of the picture. Taylor had hoped Browning or Chaney would say a word to either make her feel better or confirm her suspicions of inadequacy, but "there was none forthcoming—only frowns and looks." The director and actor continued to appear "very glum" throughout the making of the picture. This tactic must have worked, as Taylor's performance was lauded by the critics after the premiere and at least one even said she "walked away with the picture." Taylor realized later that "being discouraging is just Tod Browning's method of direction."[49]

Chaney's character was often seen wearing only a vest, which meant large amounts of make-up would be needed to simulate the suntan such an outdoorsy kind of guy would probably have. The first attempts to cover Chaney's upper body with make-up proved time consuming and ineffective, so another method would be needed. True to his reputation, Chaney opted for the physically damaging route and arranged with a local physician to bask under the searing glow of a mercury quartz lamp. Chaney achieved the effect he was looking for, but after using collodion to create the wide variety of scars "Tiger" sported from his hazardous work; the spots where he had the "scars" did not tan at the same rate the other tanned skin and required months to "bleach out."[50] Browning gave Chaney very little to work with in order to build any sort of meaningful characterization. It also appeared that Chaney was wearing some sort of back brace under his wide cummerbund and seemed rather stiff.

By now, Chaney was suffering a great deal, not only from his back and the general fatigue, but his throat was painful and irritated as well. Like the trouper he was, Chaney ignored his illness and went ahead with plans at the start of 1929 for his newest—and last silent feature—*Thunder*. The film centered around an old railroad engineer by the name of "Grumpy" Anderson, who is nearing the end of his career and having a difficult time adjusting to it. There is a subplot involving his son, who worked with him on the railroad, and a movie actress traveling by train. The film opens with a terrible blizzard which necessitated moving production out of

California. After scouting several locations, Green Bay, Wisconsin was one of the sites chosen and Chaney headed East along with Jeske to assist him. The making of *Thunder* would be fraught with complication after complication with everything from the equipment and weather to the actors themselves. Co-star James Murray had a serious problem with alcohol and required someone constantly nearby to monitor his level of intoxication. Chaney, much to his chagrin and contrary to everything he stood for, held up production for a time due to illness. His weakened physical condition made him vulnerable to a virus which laid him low for days at a time. Chaney stubbornly pushed ahead with filming and caused the virus to progress into full blown "walking" pneumonia. Even though Chaney was able to perform adequately in the part, he did require the use of a double for some of the more physically challenging shots, as well as a double to actually operate the locomotive (due to strict railroad regulations). Jeske provided the perfect choice for a double, as he had doubled for Chaney in the past, and was made up roughly to simulate Chaney's appearance. Jeske would only be seen from the back, or maybe a quick side shot, so full make-up wasn't necessary. He already had a moustache which could be easily touched up with grey to match Chaney's "old man" make-up for Grumpy. When asked about Chaney, Norma Shearer (actress and wife of MGM boss Irving Thalberg) told author Philip Riley some years later, "Lon Chaney relied heavily on his man [Jeske], more so in the last years when he was weakened by his illness. That was his assistant in *Thunder* doing the jumps. They looked very much alike."

A newspaper account from March of 1929 told a quaint story of a group of Oshkosh youths meeting their favorite actor, Lon Chaney, in a hotel lobby. One of the boys, Howard Wipl was quoted as saying: "We did not know exactly what to do or where to inquire, but finally we asked the head waiter at the hotel if anybody of the Lon Chaney party was about. She pointed out a gentleman in the lobby and told us he was the make-up man for Lon Chaney's group. We went over and talked with him. We asked him a lot of questions about Lon Chaney. We asked him how Lon Chaney looked. The make-up man shrugged his shoulders and told us he could not be sure. He said, 'If Chaney should come in now, he might be a monkey or a freak.' We knew, of course, that Chaney is the great make-up artist of the movies, and we understood what the make-up man meant. We talked there for about a half and hour, and then the elevator door opened and out stepped Lon Chaney. The make-up man called him over and told him a group of boys wanted to meet him. Chaney was very pleasant. He greeted us all as if he had known us all our lives. He did not appear a bit grumpy as he does in many of his pictures." The article goes on to state the Oshkosh boys felt very lucky to have met Chaney (who also gave each of them his autograph), considering Chaney had consistently refused to meet with other locals who congregated in the lobby on a daily basis hoping to see the movie star and get an autograph.[51]

Thunder would finally reach the theatres on July 8, 1929. By this time, Chaney's health had deteriorated to the point where the studio heads at MGM were becoming extremely nervous. It was rumored that a piece of artificial snow used in filming parts of *Thunder* lodged in Chaney's throat and caused further inflammation and allowed an infection to set in. Chaney struggled with his malady as best he could, but he could not deny the fact he was no longer able to work. Chaney had to bow out of a picture he'd been slated to star in (*The Bugle Sounds*) and was suspended by MGM from his lucrative new contract on July 25th until he was able to work again. Chaney spent the rest of the year trying to recover from this persistent illness. After a stay at a nearby spa to try to put on some of the weight he'd recently lost,[52] Chaney would finally go under the knife in September when he quietly checked into St. Vincent's Hospital to have his tonsils removed. There is a great deal of confusion and misinformation regarding the nature of Chaney's illness. One article suggested it was a cancerous tumor that was removed from Chaney's throat, not his tonsils. Whatever happened in that operating room on that September day, Chaney's condition only worsened and he began to spit up blood on an increasingly frequent basis. The situation was frightening to Chaney and especially so to Hazel who didn't understand what was going on. By October, the diagnosis was finally in—Chaney had lung cancer. There was talk of a "conspiracy of mercy" to shield Chaney from the truth, but it is very hard to believe that Chaney's doctor did not provide him with the full details of his condition. Whether Chaney shared that information with anyone but possibly his wife is unknown. Adela Rogers St. Johns records a conversation in her 1931 *Liberty Magazine* biography of Chaney between the actor and his good friend W. W. Greenwood, a MGM studio executive, where a troubled Chaney confronts his mortality: "I don't want to die. I hate going into that unknown darkness. But I can lick that. I don't want to leave my wife and my son and the babies. I love them so. What will I do without Hazel? What will she do without me? I don't want to die. I'm not ready."[53] Chaney spent about an hour with Greenwood grappling with the hard truth of his early death and his fears of what will happen to his family afterwards. As events unfold, it will be clear that Chaney had good reason to worry.

Around the time Chaney began work on his first sound film, *The Unholy Three*, in March of 1930, his second grandson was born. The child was named Ronald Creighton Chaney and his famous "grandpop" was again thrilled with the news. Chaney's fight to stay away from sound was over, and after the green light was given by an expert at the University of Southern California who administered a test of Chaney's vocal capabilities, the filming began. This was not just "business as usual," though, and Chaney was taking this latest film more seriously than he had ever done before. "I'll tell you frankly," Chaney candidly told *Photoplay* journalist Harry Lang, "that my first talking picture is going to make me or break me. Inside, I mean; in here . . . Now, listen! I hope they like my first talkie. I'm going to try my darndest to make them like it. I'm going to make it the sound picture I want, even if it takes a year to get it that way . . . If they do, that will be fine. But if they don't . . . well . . . it will do something to me. It will make me what I have never been since I went into pictures—a man whose sole interest is the money he's being paid. I'll just go ahead; making the required talkies under my contract terms, and collect my pay. And at the end of five years, I'll step out of the picture, and that will be all. I'll probably retire then, anyway. I'll have enough to take it easy."[54]

On the set, Chaney relied heavily on Jeske to help him in the dressing room. There were days when Chaney was so weak he could barely get himself together to get out on the set. Once there, he did his best not to show how ill he was, but it wasn't possible to hide the truth from everyone. Co-star Harry Earles—who had also worked with Chaney on the 1925 silent version of *The Unholy Three*—confirmed in an interview with author Michael Blake in 1985 that Chaney was noticeably ill during production and had difficulty maintaining enough strength to get through a day's worth of filming. Earles also remembered Jeske and remarked to Blake that he "bore a strong resemblance to Lon."[55]

Chaney's ventriloquist character in the film, Echo, would be required to actually perform his act in the film, in contrast to the silent version where Chaney was able to mimic certain throat movements to simulate throwing his voice. Chaney not only used a "character" voice for the dummy, but also created voices for the old lady Echo disguised himself as ("Mrs. O'Grady"); two different parrots; and a young woman in the crowd at the carnival. Chaney talked a little about sound films with a newspaper reporter and said that "on the stage we used to imitate different voices to augment disguises and this same thing will work in pictures. For instance, in the old woman's disguise in the present picture we had rather an elaborate make-up, but really got the illusion through imitation of the reedy voice of an aged person, together with walking and moving as such a person would. I think the best way to explain it is this—if you can think in the voice of the person you're playing you can speak like that person. In other words, get a mind-picture of a voice just as you do a face."[56]

The Unholy Three went on to be a great success for MGM and for Chaney personally, as his deep, masculine voice was judged to be a perfect fit for what the audience expected of him. Chaney wasn't able to fully enjoy this new success, though, as his physical condition was deteriorating rapidly. Chaney was examined by several doctors hired by MGM and based on their findings it was determined the actor was no longer able to fulfill his obligations to the studio. It was only two days later—on June 23rd—that Chaney sat down with attorney Milton Cohen and prepared what would be his Last Will and Testament. It is a very simple document, the sort of no-frills type of thing Chaney would have wanted. The main heir was, of course, his "dear, beloved wife" Hazel, who received the bulk of his estate, which was estimated at the time to be over $550,000. The only other two individuals in the will that were to receive an inheritance from Chaney's estate were ex-wife Cleva Creighton Bush (she was awarded the sum of $1.00 to prevent her from contesting the will), and his "faithful friend" John Jeske, who was to receive a sum of $5,000.00. Of Jeske, Chaney wrote into his will that his friend had "at all times been loyal to me and acted as a faithful servant . . . ." The key word here is "loyal"; a trait Chaney especially prized. Chaney's will explains that his son, Creighton, brothers John (Jonathan) and George, and sister Carrie Keyes were all previously provided for in the form of life insurance policies. The total sum of these policies was said to be around $275,000, which would then be divided four ways.

In a desperate attempt to avoid the inevitable, Lon and Hazel traveled to New York to meet with Dr. Burton J. Lee, a cancer specialist, who would examine Chaney and prescribe experimental radium treatments for his advance lung cancer. The treatments only seemed to make him weaker, and he arrived back in Los Angeles in early July to an uncertain future. Chaney's thoughts now must have been a tangled web of pain and frustration over his condition and the fact that even his incredibly strong will could not "lick" the will of God. He was dying, and he knew it.

Around July 10th, Lon, Hazel, and Jeske made the long drive to the serene mountains of Big Pine to rest and visit the brand new cabin their Los Angeles architect Paul R. Williams had designed for them (the only cabin he would ever design). This simple stone structure was built on the spot Chaney loved the most on the Palisades Glacier Road, across from his favorite fishing hole. Chaney family friend Bob Logan—owner/operator of Big Pine's Glacier Pack Train station—was mailed blue prints for the home sometime back toward the end of 1929 and set about hauling equipment, materials, and laborers up the hill by pack train to the spot where the cabin was to be constructed. Logan was not by trade a building contractor, but he was the man Chaney knew could get the job done and entrusted the project to him.[57] Long-time Big Pine resident Babe Harwood (neé Rossi) remembered when Chaney visited the site of the construction shortly before work began on *The Unholy Three*. He practiced his ventriloquism by hiding in bushes by the side of the road and "throwing" his voice to confuse the workers traveling along with the building supplies. Babe said Chaney got a big kick out of the joke, but some of the others—probably the one's who were given quite a fright by the weird voices coming out of the bushes and trees—didn't quite see the humor in it.[58]

Sadly, even a visit to his new cabin didn't help Chaney recover his strength. He was hemorrhaging several times a day now[59] and was too weak to even hold a fishing pole. Chaney sat on the porch of his "dream" cabin, or by the banks of the little stream that ran by it, and made his peace with God and man. The group was forced to return to Los Angeles early. Chaney struggled for a few weeks more to try to regain enough strength to stabilize his condition, but he was finally forced to enter the hospital on August 20th. It wasn't until this time that the public was starting to become aware of how serious Chaney's illness really was. He was given a series of blood transfusions to offset the large amount of blood he had been losing, but the damage to his lungs was irreparable. The cause of his illness was often reported as being anemia associated with a throat ailment, but Chaney's doctors knew the truth. Hazel and Creighton stayed by his side while Jeske tried his best to keep things in order at home. Chaney seemed to improve enough to eat a little bit and get some color back in his face by the 23rd—enough so for the family to have just an inkling of hope that he may actually recover. Chaney was unable to speak and fell back on the sign-language he had used to communicate with his parents. John Chaney, who lived in Los Angeles, was also at his brother's bedside for a time interpreting his signs for the hospital staff. Hazel and Creighton had learned sign-language from Chaney's father, Frank, many years earlier and were able to understand Chaney and know that he wanted them to believe he was feeling better and not to worry. Jeske drove Hazel to the hospital as always on the evening of the 26th to visit a while with her husband. He was her comforter in these difficult times and the sort of friend she needed by her side. Hazel's stepson Creighton was with his family now and becoming more and more distant from her every day. His inner demons were being stirred to the surface by the thought of his father dying and leaving him alone. Though a grown man with a wife and two sons, he still needed his "Pop"—

perhaps now more than ever to keep him focused and sane. Soon, Creighton would be like a small boat tossed about on the high seas without oar or rudder to guide him.

As with many aspects of Lon Chaney's life; the true facts of what happened the day he died are also covered with a thick layer of myth and misinformation. What is known for certain is Chaney fought the good fight as long as possible, but succumbed to his cancer at 12:55 AM on August 26, 1930.[60] Chaney's doctor, John C. Webster, was not able to reach him in time to do anything to save his famous patient. It was said that Hazel and Creighton were at his bedside when he died, but another—possibly the most accepted—story is that Chaney died alone, giving the two-fingered signal of serious distress to his nurse right before he slipped away with a smile on his face.

The funeral service two days later was meant to be a private affair with only a select group of family and close friends. The crowd outside the Cunningham and O'Conner funeral home swelled to mob dimensions and police were required to hold the unruly fans and curiosity seekers back. Inside, Chaney's pals, Sam and Jack Feinberg, wept as they played his favorite set music from behind a screen of flowers. As the strains of Chaney's beloved "Laugh, Clown, Laugh" played, Hazel became hysterical and leapt up from her seat screaming "Why! Why! Why!" before collapsing. There was a nurse at hand to attend to her. Creighton was there as well to try to offer her some support but he, too, was asking God the same question. Adela Rogers St. Johns sat next to actresses Polly Moran and Marie Dressler near the front of the chapel. She remembered from where she sat she could see Chaney in his casket with his favorite newsboy cap in his folded hands: "I wondered why we went to the funeral—and we all did—the funeral of the most private man who ever lived in Hollywood. And why we felt so deeply the loss of a man it was impossible to know well."[61] The Feinberg brothers were devastated by the loss of their good friend and benefactor. Jack Feinberg tearfully told St. Johns that Lon was "the finest man that ever lived. There will never be anybody like him. He was so kind. He loved us boys and he did everything for us. When he died, we felt like everything was ended."[62] The studio heads attended the funeral for show, mainly. St. Johns noted how they arrived twenty-five minutes late to the service and then quickly exited the chapel to their waiting limousines as soon as the last words were spoken. None of them had the courtesy to come to the cemetery to see Chaney put in his crypt at Forest Lawn Cemetery. Chaney had helped make their fortune, but his defiance of the status quo made him unpopular with some of the big boys who liked to have things their way. Chaney's star-power would be missed by the MGM executives, but not the man himself. Some of those who stayed behind at the memorial and at the graveside service went up to Jeske and offered their condolences, thinking he was Chaney's brother. The resemblance was so striking in person that it was an easy mistake to make.[63] Standing there in the group of mourners and at the casket as one of the active pallbearers, Jeske's heart was breaking at the realization he had once been so close to Chaney, yet from now on could only play the role of family servant. Jeske, like Jack Feinberg, couldn't help but feel that "everything was ended." Their whole world revolved around Chaney. Without him, they were lost.

Lon Chaney's passing touched the lives of so many people the man had helped along the way, either financially or just by listening to their troubles and giving them a hopeful word. He never announced his good deeds to the world, preferring to give in private—sometimes anonymously—to people he knew and worked with who were down on their luck or needed a helping hand to get the medical help or education they needed. Jeske was certainly one of these grateful people who was plucked from obscurity and given a chance to be more than he ever thought possible by his friend and mentor. Whatever career he thought he had at the movie studio was over—he could not betray his friend's trust by exposing the true nature of his employment—and he now focused completely on the task at hand and the promise he made to his dying friend: To take care of Hazel and be her friend and protector.

The death of a loved one can bring out the best and the worst of those closest to them, and Chaney's death was sadly no different. Creighton's fragile foothold on reality was eroding daily and Chaney's younger brother George was having personal troubles of his own. Hazel sought refuge in her own family—brother Charles and sister Eleanor Lechert—and actively sought to distance herself from her late husband's family. She would try to reach out to her stepson as best as she knew how, but her acts of kindness would eventually be for naught. Mentally and physically exhausted, Hazel desperately searched for solace in her Catholic faith as she feared the worst was soon to come.

Chapter 3:

A TIME OF TRAGEDY AND SORROW

"We felt like everything was ended."

The words of Jack Feinberg embodied the mood that permeated every facet of Hazel Chaney's world. There seemed to be no reason to go on; nothing to hope for. Hazel left the Beverly-Wilshire Residential Hotel she had taken up residence during her husband's final illness, and moved into a comfortable apartment in the quiet, residential neighborhood that once surrounded N. Hayworth Avenue. Jeske had been staying at a property Hazel was in the process of renovating on Orange Drive, but soon moved into an adjacent apartment at the stately and secure building on Hayworth. It was a far cry from the beautiful Italian-style mansion she and Chaney would have shared to begin a new phase in their lives. Chaney was just about ready to settle down a bit and enjoy some of the fruits of his heavy labors. That was all over now.

Hazel needed Jeske in her life more than ever. He was the sort of stabilizing force that was missing now that her husband was no longer by her side. She made a short visit to San Francisco to be near close friends and family, but nothing anyone said or did could diminish the pain she felt. Hazel tearfully confided to Adela Rogers St. Johns shortly after Lon's death that "[Lon] used to laugh and get embarrassed when I told him I thought he was the handsomest man in the world. And he would laugh, too, when I told him he was a great lover, far beyond any they had on the screen. But it was true. I cannot tell you how wonderful he was. Nor all the little things he did for me always."[1] At this point Hazel broke down and sobbed, unable to continue the interview. Her loss was so deep—so inexorable—there was no way to console her.

Perhaps it was this overwhelming feeling that her life, too, had ended that pushed Hazel to immediately make plans to dispose of many of the things she and Chaney had held very dear. The fantastic mansion in Beverly Hills she and Lon had planned every inch of and selected every material and piece of furniture for was up for sale. Chaney's make-up kit—the source of materials for so many of his wondrous transformations—was donated to the Natural History Museum in Los Angeles along with costumes and devices from *The Penalty* and other films. Though Creighton agreed to the donation on the surface, inside he was hurt at the thought his father's magnificent make-up case and other personal artifacts did not go to him. Instead, he received the small case made out of a metal lunch box his father had used in his early days at Universal. Somehow, this wasn't quite enough.

The mansion on Whittier Drive sold on February 22nd to a Mr. and Mrs. Frank Hann who promptly announced their intention to add two bedrooms an additional servant's quarters to the original home. It was reported the Hann's purchased the Chaney's dream house and property for $80,000.[2] Hazel was cashing in as much property and other investments as she could, but why? Was it as a hedge against the costs of maintaining her lifestyle? She had received more than enough from Lon's estate to keep her very comfortable, so this seems unlikely. Was she liquidating the estate to make it easier to keep under her complete control? Possibly. Hazel was creating a wall between herself and the Chaney family for what appears to be her own protection. Jeske was not only her comforter and friend, but an ally in her business affairs. He became her personal secretary and handled her correspondence and many of her business transactions. Chaney's personal secretary, his old friend Phil Epstein, bowed out of Hollywood after Lon's death. There was a partnership forming between Jeske and Lon's widow built upon Hazel's desperation and fears over her own declining health. There was also genuine affection between them, as they both needed a friend during this sad time and could understand each other's sorrow. The loss of Chaney at the prime of his life bonded the two of them, and yet the tragedy only seemed to serve as a wedge between Hazel and her stepson, Creighton.

For many years Creighton had suppressed his great desire to follow in his father's footsteps and become a motion picture actor. He had taken small parts in high school productions, and felt he had what it takes to make it the dog-eat-dog world of show business. Unfortunately for him, his father thought otherwise. Chaney had a deep-seated fear that his son was weak; the same weakness he saw in Creighton's mother. Chaney did what he knew best to "make a man" out of his boy, and sometimes his methods were a bit too harsh, too old-fashioned, but they were necessary in the father's mind. Years later Creighton would cry in his cups that his father beat him and displayed a touch of sadism in his treatment of his sensitive son. Full details of this story have yet to surface.[3] Creighton loved and respected his father deeply, yet at the same time he resented him with a passion for keeping him from his mother for so many years, and never encouraging his desire to work in the movie business. Now that Chaney was dead and buried, the son felt free to pursue his dream no matter what the costs.

Hazel knew of her stepson's wish, and though fully aware of her late husband's sentiments on the subject, she agreed to do what she could to help. Chaney once told his close friend W. W. Greenwood, "I just don't want my son in this business. Maybe he'd survive. Most of them don't. It's a crazy racket. You know that. I'd been through hell and back before I got into it, so it didn't upset me much. Besides, I could afford to stay away from most of it. The kid's different. I want to keep him out of Hollywood. I'm not afraid he'd be a failure. I'm afraid he'd be a success. I'd rather he'd be a good plumber than a movie star."[4] Hazel was able to call in a few favors and have Creighton invited to various studio parties to get to know the casting directors and others who were in a position to hire the inexperienced young man with the famous name. Early in 1931, while the naïve Creighton was at one of these parties being ogled by the group of seasoned studio veterans, an assistant director, with probably more than a few drinks in him, casually tossed out the nugget, "You're Lon Chaney's son. You ought to be in pictures!" Creighton quipped "How about it?" and the director promised to have a job for him in a couple days. Flushed with optimism, Creighton promptly gave notice to his father-in-law and quit the water heater business to pursue his acting career. It didn't occur to the young man at the time that he didn't have an acting career, nor did he have any real prospects for employment at the studio. Seven months went by and no call from the studio offering the fabulous job, and the assistant director who had made his extravagant comment was suddenly "unavailable" whenever Creighton called. Money was running out and his marriage was becoming strained. Creighton had given all the money from his father's life insurance policy to his wife Dorothy to put in a trust fund for their two boys. Dorothy was a very smart woman, and she could see her husband was on a collision course with financial ruin. She acted swiftly to ensure that Creighton could not get his hands on any of the money, and used a good deal of it to keep her father's water heater business afloat during the very difficult time of the Depression. In time, her investment would pay off a hundred-fold and provide a small fortune to herself, the children, and her father.

Desperate for money, Creighton went to Hazel to demand some of his father's inheritance he felt was rightly his own. Creighton was a big man with something of a temper who could easily intimidate the frightened, tiny woman. In response, Hazel retreated further and further into her own world surrounded by her brother Charles Bennett and his wife Maud. Sister Eleanor Lechert and her sons were there to comfort her as well. Hazel brought her mother Louise down from San Francisco after her father's death and set her up in a small house on Waring Avenue. With her family and Jeske by her side, she felt better able to deal with the demands of the Chaney family. The one ally on her husband's side of the family was his step-mother, Cora. Hazel and Lon had been providing monthly financial aid to help her pay the bills after Frank Chaney's death. Hazel and Jeske would often visit Cora and talk about the sad state of affairs. Sometimes, Cora's niece, Joy V. Parker, was there and would join in the conversation. Joy was a large, friendly woman with a hard edge to her that hinted at her fundamentally callous and greedy nature. She was married to a man named Lynden Parker (sometimes spelled "Linden" or "Lynnden") whom she met back in his home town of Ft. Wayne, Indiana. They moved to Los Angeles around 1920 along with Lynden's mother Mary, brother Murel and sister Pansy and their families, and another sister named Mabel.

Joy and Lynden were childless, but before long, Joy's two teenage daughters from her first marriage—Marie and Joan—would arrive from Michigan to further complicate the already-overcrowded living conditions.[5] Joy enjoyed her tenuous connection to the famous Lon Chaney family and milked it for whatever she could get. She soon worked herself into Hazel's good graces and was able to gain her confidence. Joy eyed Jeske with contempt and wanted him out of the way. For now, though, she would maintain a cordial relationship with Jeske so as not to alert Hazel's suspicions that her attention was anything more than a kind concern for her dead relative's widow.

On May 2, 1931, the first of what would be four installments of the biography of Lon Chaney, written by Adela Rogers St. Johns, was published in *Liberty* magazine. Though intended as a magazine article, it was a ground-breaking work in the field of Chaney biography that would not be attempted again until the 1970s. Her sympathetic and sometimes emotional writing style was often ridiculed by her colleagues in the male dominated field of journalism, but her biography of Chaney has proven to be quite reliable and revealing. St. Johns would go on to enjoy an amazingly productive, award-winning, and influential career in journalism until her death in 1988. In 1931, St. Johns was still working hard to prove herself and saw in Chaney an opportunity to use her skills to tell the "real" story of her friend's life—not the Hollywood myth machine's version. It was in this first installment that the name "John Jeske"—the "devoted friend and servant"—was mentioned in connection with Chaney for the first time. St. Johns had witnessed firsthand how Jeske worked with Chaney on his make-up and as a stand-in at the studio on many occasions and knew of Jeske's important role in the Chaney household. She told how Jeske, "chauffeur extraordinaire and prime minister for the unseen Mrs. Chaney," would appear ready to go at the stroke of five o'clock to take his boss home for dinner. It wasn't until the next week's article that the revelation came that "Jeske was always in Lon's dressing room" and told of the close friendship and personal resemblance the two men shared. The articles only fanned the flames of Creighton's jealous hatred of Jeske and set the stage for an even greater tragedy to come.

Jeske was flattered by all the attention, but uncomfortable in the spotlight. He couldn't help but have his head turned a little bit, though, and he indulged his desire for the finer things with the large sum of money he had been given by Chaney in his will. Jeske was a man with an artistic eye for design and he adorned himself in some very stylish new suits. His moustache was trimmed to the very latest pencil-thin style. Jeske made the mistake of carrying around large sums of money and "accidentally on purpose" displayed the roll of bills whenever he made a purchase. He fed his ego at the expense of his own personal safety. There were eyes watching him that would be plotting his downfall. The clock was ticking and time would not be on Jeske's side.

Elaine Beuter, the ambitious young lady Jeske had met on the grounds of MGM, had divorced her ad-executive husband and moved back to Los Angeles hoping to rekindle her screenwriting career. Just before the divorce, she had written a lengthy confession to her husband Paul's father telling him of her unhappiness and how the disintegration of the marriage was her own fault. She said she wanted to write the letter so he would "understand a bit that is the real Elaine": "Hollywood has ruined me . . . Once its poison got into my soul, it has forever stained it. I love my Hollywood with a folly and passion that holds no rhyme or reason . . . I have sought in the best way I know to put it from my mind, but my heart is rebellion, and I realize I am quite a little fool." She ends her letter with the statement: "I am not as frivolous as you might be led to believe, neither am I as cold and selfish as you might think. I am only trying to find for both of us, the minimum of happiness which all the world seeks." For his part, Paul Beuter would later describe this matrimonial interlude with Elaine bluntly as being a '"stupid marriage."[6] The studio doors were not opening wide at the return of "Elaine Wilmont," and for now, she turned once again to her mother Gertrude for comfort and a place to stay. No doubt the newspaper reports that Jeske had inherited $5,000 from Chaney and the *Liberty* articles were read with great interest by the two women. Plans were being made for a reunion.

The first anniversary of Chaney's death was going to be an especially hard one for everyone involved. With the rise of sound films, the Feinberg brothers, Sam and Jack, found themselves closer and closer to redundancy, and they were barely hanging on to their jobs at MGM. Jack still lived with his parents and brother Sam was married, but childless. The death of Chaney seemed to hit Sam especially hard and he had been in a state of severe depression since that horrible day in 1930. About a week before the anniversary of his friend's death—August 14th—Sam was driving to work as usual. He was a little late getting started that morning; perhaps a bit preoccupied with thoughts of impending unemployment and the loss of Chaney. There was a long line of cars stopped at an intersection to allow the Pacific Electric rail car to pass and Sam was forced to stop and wait. No one knows what the motivation really was for what happened next, all that is known is Sam Feinberg applied the gas to his large sedan and quickly made his way around the parked cars and on to the railroad tracks. Within seconds, the car was struck by the train, crushing the front end and passenger compartment, and dragging it for nearly 100 feet before the train could be forced to a halt. He died instantly. It took nearly an hour for emergency personnel to free the car from the train and remove Sam's body.[7] There was no follow-up word in the press from Jack about the loss of his beloved brother, but one can surmise that his grief was beyond words—beyond comprehension. Was Sam's death an unfortunate accident or a suicide? We will never know for sure.

It wasn't long before tragedy struck again close to the Chaney home. Jeske had severed most of the ties with his family for reasons known only to him, but he maintained a connection to his older brother Gus. Gus was still working with his brother Julius at the Jeske Brothers Bakery in Scranton, Pennsylvania, and doing the best he could to stay out of the hornet's nest of troubles Julius and his family were always surrounded in. Julius' family had swelled to ten children and he found it increasingly hard to make ends meet in a business hard hit by the Depression. He turned to the bottle even more now as an escape from his burdens and became increasingly violent at home with his frightened wife and daughters. His only surviving son, Julius, Jr., married a nice Polish girl and was getting ready to settle down when the bottom fell out of their world. In the wee hours of November 7th, Julius staggered home in the freezing cold from a local speakeasy at the corner of Prospect

Avenue and Cherry Street after a long night of heavy drinking. He was only a block away from his home when he slipped on the ice and fell hard to the ground. The left side of his face connected with the cement curb and cracked his skull. Julius was still semi-conscious when he was found by a passerby and was taken straight away to his house and placed on the couch in the front parlor. His eye socket was crushed and the eyeball hung from a strand of flesh. Julius Jr., Mrs. Jeske, and the other children gathered around him and begged him to go to the hospital. Still under the influence of alcohol, Julius shouted angrily that he would not go to the hospital, and the family obeyed his wishes. They knew better than to cross him, even at a time like this. Julius soon lost consciousness and died around 5 a.m. Though a tyrant at home, Julius was a well-respected member of the business community in Scranton, and his funeral was attended by many prominent South Scranton business people and members of the Christ Lutheran Church where Julius and his family worshipped. The Junger Maennershor chorus—the elder Julius had been a member—sang as his casket was lowered into the ground. His widow and orphans found themselves evicted from their home and the bakery was closed down. They made due in a small apartment a few blocks away. Mrs. Jeske and the children old enough to work found odd jobs here and there to make ends meet. Julius, Jr. was fortunate to find work in another local bakery and Gus eventually went to work in one of the many coal mines in the Scranton area. Gus' lungs were already severely damaged from breathing the mountains of flour dust over the years, so working in a coal mine only exacerbated his physical decline. Julius Jeske's sad legacy has been the psychological destruction of his family and a lasting memory of his cruelty and abuse.[8] There were a few good memories too from the early days, like his generosity during World War I in sending a train car full of food to Europe to help the starving civilians. The death of his beloved first wife Christine and infant daughter Polina in 1917 and his son George in 1929, seemed to snap whatever link to humanity he had left and he lashed out at the world. It's no wonder his younger brothers chose to keep their distance from all this pain and suffering, but word did reach John in California in that dark November about his brother's accident and death.

Deeply troubled by the news, Jeske sent Gus some money to help the family out, and wrote a letter to his youngest niece, Freda, who was 14 years old. There is nothing but Freda's word to document this incident, but it appears that Jeske was trying to find a way to bring her out to California to live in order to reduce the financial burden on his brother's widow, Adele. It is easy to believe that a soft-hearted woman like Hazel, who often opened her pocket book to many disadvantaged people through her husband, Lon, would have been willing to set up a trust account for Freda and see to it she had a good home and education. Freda bravely decided to remain in Scranton to help her mother during this terrible time, but gladly accepted her Uncle John's financial aid.

Hazel tried to maintain the beautiful new mountain cabin in Big Pine as long as she could, but in 1932 she made the difficult decision to sell. She hadn't been feeling well for a long time. The debilitating fatigue limited her daily activities and she feared the worst. She knew how Lon had suffered and she could see herself becoming ill the same way he did. Hazel was terrified. One of the people she trusted to handle some of her investments was a man of German ancestry named Ruluff Slimmer. Slimmer (who was 52 years old at the time) and his wife had enjoyed being guests of the Chaney's on more than one of their mountain vacations. He agreed to purchase the cabin from Hazel. Jeske handled all the paperwork and followed Slimmer to the cabin to finalize the agreement. The two men would maintain a cordial relationship for many years.

Creighton was again furious about the sale, believing the cabin should have been rightly his. His fury was mixed with shame, as he had to explain time and again why so much of his father's estate was not passed on to his only natural son. In interviews given a few years later, Creighton fabricated stories of how his father had died penniless to explain the lack of an inheritance, or rather the inheritance he no longer had control of. The situation would only get worse for Creighton in the days ahead. His drinking was increasing steadily and he started having meaningless affairs with pretty studio fluff he found in large supply. The young would-be actor was finally offered a contract by RKO pictures supposedly after the assistant director who had originally promised him a job had an attack of conscience and helped the younger Chaney by introducing him to a casting director at RKO. The studio had wanted Creighton to use the name "Lon Chaney, Jr." but for now, the son refused. Creighton didn't feel he was entitled to take his father's name—he wasn't an actor yet. The contract paid Creighton $200.00 a week and had him steadily employed in bit parts in B and C westerns. The studio seemed unsure of how to promote their new "find." While Creighton was mainly riding horses and being the "heavy" in westerns, RKO paid for a series of promotional "beefcake" shots of the aspiring actor working out with a trainer on the roof of the Hollywood Athletic Club. These photos were an attempt to appeal to the predominantly female readership of such fan magazines as *Screen Romances*. The large, awkward young actor was not cut out to be a heartthrob and this promotion went nowhere.

After a visit to her doctor's office in October of 1932, Hazel was given the traumatic news that she had breast cancer. The source of her fatigue and general malaise was finally located, but somehow she had known all along. Nothing could be done, but to wait and see how quickly the disease would progress. Jeske was shaken to his core by this unexpected new tragedy. Why had Hazel been struck down so soon with this horrible disease that had taken Lon? What would become of *him* if Hazel died? There was no time to wallow in self-pity or shake fists at God. Jeske did what he could, as he always did, to comfort Hazel and work even more diligently and quickly to make the final arrangements for disposing of her large estate. The holiday season would again be a very somber time.

Even the weather seemed different as 1933 rolled around. The days melted into summer without the usual spike in temperatures—it was unnaturally cool for a Los Angeles summertime. Any real heat in the air was being generated on the labor front where scores of workers took to the streets in protest. Hundreds—maybe thousands—of people were out of a job because of the Depression and relying heavily on Roosevelt's new welfare system. The city of Los Angeles—especially due to its lure of a glamorous Hollywood lifestyle—attracted more than its fair share of young drifters and vagabonds from all over the country hoping to find a better life. Even travel brochures of the day warned people not to come to the city if they were expecting to find work. There wasn't enough employment to go around, and those without a job existed on the fringes looking for anyway to make a buck. Some even resorted to illegal means to pay their bills. Across town from the plush neighborhood where Hazel and Jeske lived, the lives of the average person were very different. Each day was a struggle to make it through to the next. Cora Chaney's niece Joy Parker and her husband Lynden lived in a poverty-stricken area of East Los Angeles. Lynden made a meager living working at the Willys-Overland manufacturing plant, and doing some body work and vehicle painting on the side. He took whatever job he could and sometimes took money under the table for jobs stripping or altering vehicles for underworld thugs. Joy didn't care what Lynden did for a living as long as he they had food on the table and a roof over her head. She got a thrill out of being a sort of den mother to a group of young punks who hung around her husband's shop. Now and then she'd help one of them out with a few bucks to pay their rent or whatever else was needed. The gifts were not out of the goodness of her heart, though, and had heavy strings attached.

One of the young men befriended by the Parker's was Floyd Britton, a jaded 24-year-old with a wife and baby son he couldn't care less about. He had recently been one of the many who labored long and hard to create Boulder Dam, and was cited for his heroism in rescuing a fellow worker who hung precariously from a ledge. That seemed like such a long time ago now. Britton—who was known as "Jimmy" to the gang—was too busy these days hanging out with his buddies and thinking up petty crimes to commit in order to get enough money to buy illegal booze and other contraband. Prohibition had just been repealed in 1933, so the market for bootleg liquor was drying up. Cheap liquor was always in demand, so the profits were there for the taking if you knew how to work the system, and didn't ask too many questions. Britton found Cyril Russell, a former Army buddy, a malleable accomplice. He was a few years older than Britton, but not nearly as street wise. Russell—nicknamed "Heavy" due to his large size—was a farm boy who knew very little about big city life. He had come to Los Angeles like all the others to find his fortune, but only found disappointment and poverty. A 25-year-old with a long criminal record, Jerry Lamaroux, who went by the alias "George Dorsey," rounded out the little gang. On the fringes was a troubled young woman named Ida Mae Alameda who lived with Britton in a small apartment on Main Street they shared with Russell. Ida Mae had run away from her Northern California home in the small coastal town of Ft. Bragg at fourteen and made her way by train to Los Angeles. Her father had abandoned the family when Ida was ten years of age. A couple years later, Ida helped to supplement her family's meager income by picking berries after school. By sixteen, she was working as a waitress in a small café in Los Angeles when she met Britton. In an account of her life written years later, Ida would describe herself as "having fallen practically from the cradle into one grand mess." She knew Britton was married, but he told her the usual story about his wife not understanding him and he would leave her soon. At the ripe old age of twenty, Ida Mae was still too stupid— or was it the simple fact she loved him—to see through the good-looking young man's lies, and wanted very much to believe she and Britton would eventually be married. Joy and Lynden kept them under their control by frequent trips over the county line to purchase cheap alcohol and parties on the beach into the wee hours. They drank heavily, boasting about all the crimes they've committed or were about to commit. During the day there was nothing to do and nowhere to go and nothing better to hope for tomorrow. The world was a bleak place indeed if you were not one of Tinsel Town's elite.

October began with a record heat wave. The sweltering citizens of Los Angeles County—as well as most of the West Coast—saw temperatures reaching 100 degrees. The lack of humidity and high heat exacerbated what would be known as the "Griffith Park Fire" of October 3, 1933. Acres were scorched and blackened and many men who worked to contain the blaze were killed. Large crews of welfare workers were on the mountain that day to help clear brush when the fire mysteriously started. After it was all over, 29 workers were reported killed and over 150 injured. In the midst of the heat and devastating fire, Hazel was struggling with her own pain and suffering. She knew she had less time than even her doctor's hinted at. The cancer had metastasized to her lungs and liver. There was no more time to make plans and distribute her wealth as she wanted. Hazel no longer had the strength to fight and looked to her faithful companion Jeske to help finalize the plans she had been so carefully putting into place ever since her beloved husband died. She had an idea—a wild, improbable idea—to see that her estate would be distributed exactly as she wanted after her death and also avoid having to pay the high priced lawyers' fees and go through a lengthy probate. The idea never seemed like a good one, but what else could she do? Hazel firmly believed she was between that proverbial rock and a hard place and could see no other way out of her predicament.

It was another warmer-than-usual morning on that particular Saturday, October 14th. Jeske drove the big sedan down to the courthouse. He parked the car and made his way up the steps to the marriage license bureau where a clerk sat behind the window. Jeske was feeling nervous. He had been asked to do a lot of things in the past and had never felt a twinge of apprehension before, but now he found himself in one of the most awkward positions of his entire life. Jeske approached the window and asked the clerk for two blanks to file a notice of intention to marry. The clerk, Rosamond Rice, eyed the slightly built, dark-complexioned man with suspicion and asked why his fiancée wasn't with him. Jeske was afraid to say too much in the crowded courthouse, and began to write his name down on a piece of paper to give to the clerk. As he reached across the desk, he had a change of heart and put the paper back in his coat pocket. He finally managed to tell the clerk his fiancée is Mrs. Hazel Chaney and she is gravely ill in the hospital and could not appear at the courthouse. Jeske further stated that he was Mrs. Chaney's chauffeur. Miss Rice claims that she "told the man that if he would get a doctor's certificate of her illness, a notice could be filed and a license issued in three days. He took away a blank with him, saying he was going to the hospital to have Mrs. Chaney fill it out. I told him he would have to return by Noon with the papers." The clerk watched Jeske walk away from her window and waited until he rounded the corner before picking up the phone to call St. Vincent's Hospital and ask to speak to Hazel's doctor, Dr. C. G. Toland, who gave her information regarding Hazel's condition and the chauffeur's name: "John Jeske." Miss Rice was told by the doctor that "he had heard of talk about the marriage as a means of rewarding Jeske for his long and faithful services in the Chaney household, but there were family objections."[9]

There were definitely "family objections," but on which side of the family—or was it both sides—it is not clear. Thanks to the nosey courthouse clerk, news of the proposed marriage and Hazel's serious illness were plastered across newspapers from coast to coast. What had been hoped for as a simple and painless solution to a problem exploded into an even bigger mess than anyone could have anticipated. The news hounds greedily grabbed hold of the story and quickly turned it into a sordid tale of an illicit affair between the hired hand and the boss' wife. In this case, the "boss" had been the great Lon Chaney, star of the silver screen and master make-up artist who had only died a short three years prior. Was this an ongoing affair, the gossip-hungry public mused? Tongues wagged and reputations were being destroyed by the hour. Hazel was beside herself with anguish over the leak of her secret plans to the press, and her family demanded to know what was happening. A dazed and irritated Creighton was approached by reporters for his reaction and hopefully to dig up more dirt on the "affair."

"I know absolutely nothing about this marriage plan," Creighton angrily snapped back to the reporter, "You'll have to ask Mr. Jeske about that. I have not been able to see my mother for several weeks. I am told, due to her illness." He then stormed off, refusing to answer any further questions.[10] The stepson was kept away from Hazel's hospital room, yet her sister Eleanor, brother Charles, and Jeske visited her bedside every day to cheer her up and take care of any business. It wasn't Hazel's illness that kept Creighton away. He must have known that.

Jeske turned to Chaney family friend and tax attorney, Claude I. Parker,[11] for help. Parker, his law partner Ralph W. Smith, and general attorney George Koster, had been retained by Hazel after she dismissed her personal attorney Milton Cohen. It is not known why Hazel felt the need to change attorneys, but it is most likely the fact that she wanted full control of the affairs of the estate and needed lawyers with the utmost expertise in the area of inheritance taxes. Her main confidant was Parker, who had been a guest at the Chaney home with his wife Cathryn on many occasions. Now, Parker was called into the forefront to help mediate this unfortunate misunderstanding. At Jeske's request, he went to the hospital to talk to Hazel about her illness and the marriage plan. Hazel knew her idea had seriously backfired and she was forced to fall back on the legality of a formal will to dispose of her estate. Parker and Smith put the final touches on her Last Will and Testament and had Hazel sign the document on October 17, 1933. Also on that day, Parker addressed the news media and issued a statement: "I was permitted to see Mrs. Chaney for a short time. She agreed with me that, at least until she recovers from her illness, if she recovers, it will be best to forego the marriage." The reporters clamored for news about Jeske, and Parker revealed that he was "grief stricken" by all the negative press and sordid comments regarding the proposed marriage, and he was in seclusion in an undisclosed location in the Hollywood area and off limits to reporters desperate for an interview. Parker added that Jeske "joined with Mrs. Chaney in the decision to postpone [the] marriage plans."[12]

It was at this time that the amazing assertion of Jeske having been Lon Chaney's "make-up man" appeared in print for the first time. The idea seems to have been reported by some Associated Press journalist and picked up over the wire by virtually every other newspaper across the country. Since Jeske immediate went into hiding after the fiasco at the courthouse and avoided the press like the plague, who was it that made this extraordinary claim? *The Lincoln Star* stated very matter-of-factly that "Jeske was [Lon] Chaney's most trusted friend and it was he who served as the noted character actor's make-up man." The article continued on to state how "friends say that since the death of Chaney, Jeske had been a frequent companion of Mrs. Chaney and has assisted her in the management of the estate left her by the actor."[13] Did the AP reporter talk to some of Chaney's colleagues at the movie studio who knew of Jeske's involvement with Chaney's make-up work? Was it a family "friend" who knew of Jeske's work that gave away his secret? One thing is for certain: Jeske kept his mouth firmly shut.

Incredibly, while all of this drama was swirling around him, Jeske had gotten back together with Elaine Beuter and they were secretly seeing each other whenever his schedule would allow. Elaine's mother had been able to get her daughter a job as a stenographer at the movie studio where she worked as a set draper. The mother and daughter shared a modest home on Citrus Avenue, not far from the apartment building where Jeske and Hazel Chaney lived. Jeske's affection for the Elaine blinded him to the more reckless and irresponsible side of her personality. She drank too much; partied too much; and had an aversion to boredom of any kind. She was looking for the fast life again, and she thought Jeske—with his ties to the Chaney's and MGM—would be her ticket to the high-life. There was even a small resemblance between Jeske and her ex-husband Paul Beuter. The resemblance would turn out to be more than just physical, as both men desired a stable home life with a woman who wanted nothing more than to be a dutiful wife. Elaine was hardly of that temperament. She needed excitement and an outlet for her creative energies. Right now, though, she needed cash—and lots of it.

Hazel must have known about Jeske's love for Elaine. Why would he agree to Hazel's marriage plan if he wanted to marry Elaine? It is probable there would have been a loophole for him in the plan somewhere, since Hazel and Jeske knew full well the marriage would be in name only. There was no romance between them, no great affair, simply a deep understanding that went beyond the flesh and bound them tightly together. Jeske's fierce loyalty to Lon and Hazel would have compelled him to do whatever was asked if it meant preserving their legacy in some way. The two knew full well Hazel was going to die soon, so the marriage could never be consummated. They also knew Jeske had his own plans to marry Elaine. It was all such a crazy, tangled, mess, but Hazel's troubles would be over soon. Jeske's were only just beginning.

On October 31, 1931, Hazel Chaney died in her bed at St. Vincent's Hospital; the same hospital where her husband Lon had died only three years before. Hazel's family—Eleanor and Charles—and Jeske were there when she passed away. Before she expired, Hazel gave Jeske a diamond ring valued at approximately $8,000, and other personal items. She knew the estate would be plunged into a lengthy probate process that could take years to resolve due to the intricacies of the financial planning. Jeske had very little money of his own, and needed ready cash to help pay the bills and make a fresh start in life. He had been a little too free with the money Lon gave him—new clothes, a brand new blue, Ford V8 3-window coupe, and, of course, pricey gifts for his demanding girlfriend. Life wasn't going to be easy for him on any level, and Hazel tried to alleviate the immediate financial crisis by giving him expensive items that could be quickly sold off for cash. Her largess would prove to be a magnet attracting all the low-life parasites who had attached themselves to the Chaneys.

There was very little press attention given to Hazel's death. No flowing tributes or lengthy biographies. Most of the obituaries that did appear in print strangely failed to mention her stepson, Creighton, though Jeske figured prominently as the grieving ex-fiancé. Short shrift was given to Lon Chaney.

Preparations had all been made while Hazel was still alive and Jeske and Hazel's family made sure her last wishes were carried out to the letter. Last rites were read for Hazel at her beloved St. Ambrose Catholic Church on North Fairfax Avenue the morning of November 3rd.[14] Father O'Toole conducted the requiem mass. That evening, at 8:30 p.m., a rosary was said for Hazel at the Cunningham and O'Connor funeral home, where her husband had been eulogized and mourned. There were only a handful of people there to say goodbye to a woman so few knew really well, and the ones who did remained silent. Jeske was there, sitting off to the side, once again suffering through the loss of another close friend and benefactor. Joy Parker was also there, sitting next to Hazel's deeply bereaved mother, Louise. She poured her heart out to Joy about the daughter she adored and the sadness she could hardly bear. Hazel, by all accounts, was a strong, intelligent, woman with a good heart who loved her husband deeply and lived only to see him happy and prosperous in whatever he did. She would not have loved Lon less if he had quit the acting business and gone back to wallpaper hanging, just as long as they were content and had what they needed to get by. Hazel liked nice things, and toward the end of Lon's life, finally indulged herself a little (with his full approval) and purchased expensive fur coats and jewelry. It was going to finally be their time to live it up. She and Lon had paid such a heavy price all those years ago to make their dream come true. Hazel never did recover from the shock of losing Lon and all they had hoped for together. Death released her from the suffering and grief and was a welcome visitor.

The will Hazel had prepared with Parker and Smith was filed on November 8th and quickly made headlines across the country. With Hazel's complicated financial plan, the document is lengthy and detailed in its attempt to be definitive and uncontestable. The will provided for a group of main inheritors of the estate and a number of recipients of annuities Hazel had set-up during her lifetime. The individuals most prominently named as Hazel's beneficiaries are family members—Eleanor Grace Bennett Lechert, Louise Bennett, Charles Bennett's wife Maude, and her siblings' children. The only non-Bennett family members mentioned as beneficiaries were Cora Chaney and John Jeske. Creighton's name is mentioned one time in the second clause: "I declare I am the surviving widow of my late beloved husband, Lon F. Chaney, and that I have no child or children; that by a former marriage my late husband left surviving him one child, to wit, Creighton Chaney." As a further embarrassment to Creighton, not only did Hazel completely disinherit him, she also included a clause—much like her late-husband had in his will to discourage Creighton's mother Cleva from making a claim on his estate—which stated to the effect that if anyone tries to contest the will in any way, their sole compensation will be a grand total of one dollar. In razor-sharp contrast, Jeske became the recipient of $10,000 cash, numerous personal items such as linen, tableware, and furniture, as well as a portfolio of stocks and bonds and real property. Hazel went even further to stipulate that after all the other provisions of her will were carried out, an additional legacy totaling no more than $15,000 should also be given to Jeske. Even in the serious, legal language of a last will and testament, Hazel's words for Jeske come through with warmth and sincerity: "This benefit is made in grateful memory of the deep friendly affection and esteem which my late husband and I have held fast for this cherished and dependable friend for many years." For Jeske, it was a bittersweet tribute and an exceptionally generous inheritance from a woman he had come to know as an intimate friend.

Hazel had already provided for her brother Charles and mother Louise by purchasing homes for them in the West Hollywood area.

Sister Eleanor was given a home on Vista Street in the will along with a fur coat and some expensive jewelry—including a dazzling diamond wrist watch marked on the reverse with the name "Hazel." Maude Bennett was bequeathed the piano she had wanted for her daughter Genevieve. St. Ambrose Catholic Church was to receive $500 as a token of Hazel's appreciation. Charles and Eleanor's children, Louise Bennett, and Cora Chaney would all receive annuities which were designed to provide monthly income for life. Hazel tried to think of everything, but what she didn't plan for was the wrath of her slighted stepson, Creighton.

Creighton exploded with a fury over the pain of abandonment and rejection he was feeling over losing his father's estate—it was *his* legacy. None of it should end up in the hands of some filthy foreigner like Jeske. Creighton confronted Jeske spewing forth a stream of obscenities and threats, hoping to put the "family servant" in his proper place. The stepson knew it was Jeske's idea to marry Hazel on her deathbed just for this reason—to get her money. He was sure of it, since he believed all Germans were shifty, criminal types. Jeske did his best to calm the young man down and talk some sense into him, but it only partially worked. Creighton backed down for now, but he was seething inside and wanted revenge—a complete, and utter revenge like he had perpetrated not that long ago on all those high school bullies who set out to make his life miserable. It is easy to imagine he ran through scenarios in his mind of ways to make Jeske pay. Creighton next barged into the offices of Claude Parker and Ralph W. Smith and argued with them for hours about Hazel's will and threatened to drag it into the courts for a lengthy legal battle.

Buried in a small newspaper out of Illinois, an article appeared on November 2nd claiming to have the true story behind the failed marriage plans: "Motives behind the intended marriage of John Jeske and Mrs. Lon Chaney were placed in a new light today when close friends revealed it was at her express wish that Jeske sought a marriage license two weeks before her death. Mrs. Chaney desired a death-bed marriage with her chauffeur in order to prevent unfriendly relatives of her late husband, the great character actor, from obtaining any of her wealth, friends said. Jeske only consented to serve as intermediary so that her inheritance would pass into the hands of her own relatives."[15] A Nevada newspaper echoed this theme by stating that "friends later explained Mrs. Chaney desired a deathbed marriage with her husband's trusted employee to assure the disposal of her large estate to close relatives."[16] How many people knew of the strife that existed between Hazel and the Chaney family since Lon's death? Could the trouble have been brewing even before Lon passed away? The answer is most likely in the affirmative, but there is no written evidence left for public scrutiny except for these fascinating newspaper clippings.

Hollywood gossip diva Louella Parsons was known for her acerbic tongue and penchant for ruining the careers of those she didn't especially like. It is even more implausible, then, she would publish a defense of Jeske in her nationally syndicated newspaper column, *Movie Go-Round*: "Mrs. Lon Chaney, widow of one of the most successful character screen actors of his time, was followed to the grave by John Jeske, faithful friend and servant. Despite all rumors to the contrary, that is just what John Jeske was—faithful friend. When he applied for a marriage license to wed Mrs. Chaney tongues started wagging. Jeske thought by marrying Mrs. Chaney he could carry out her last bequests. There never was a romance between them. He was her friend and the friend of Lon Chaney and his one mission in life was to see that Mrs. Chaney's last moments were free from worry."[17] Quite an extraordinary collection of words from someone more likely to tear a person down than try to build them up. Was Jeske behind this? Someone very close to Hazel most definitely was, and it's probably safe to assume Jeske used Parsons' column to make his side of the story known. It was a rather awkward (but heartfelt) attempt to redeem himself and restore Hazel's reputation. Too bad so few people read Parsons' column that day, and those who did seemed to prefer the more lurid, but completely fabricated, story of a sordid affair born from greed.

Attorney's Parker and Smith gathered together Charles Bennett, Eleanor Lechert, and John Jeske in December of 1933 for a hasty meeting to discuss amending the will to include a portion of inheritance to go to Creighton Chaney. The three beneficiaries agreed to give Creighton what he wanted and avoid an ugly scene in public over the Chaney estate. The agreement gave the stepson a large number of his father's personal effects: household items, furniture, fishing rods, a Lincoln automobile, and $2,500 cash. It was also decided Hazel's gift to St. Ambrose Church was not valid and therefore rescinded, but no reason for this action was given in the court documents.

Many of the Chaney estate's personal items were still in storage in various places around town. Lon's fishing rods and gear were in the garage of Eleanor Lechert's new home on Vista Street. Some of the furniture was located at Louis Mansey's house on Laurel Avenue. No one could get their hands on anything until the will made it through the courts, and it would appear the process would drag on for years, even with Creighton taken care of. A furniture maker, Charles S. Lane, brought a suit against the estate to pay for a dining room set Hazel had ordered along with many other expensive items for the mansion she and Lon were to move into before his death. For some reason, the dining room set valued at $1,448 was never paid for. Parker and Smith took care of the bill out of the estate requiring yet another adjustment to the amount bequeathed to the others and reams of paperwork.

Jeske tried to take care of all the last minute business diligently and responsibly, but the cash was running low. He paid off Hazel's remaining bills—small items like paying off the milk man, phone bills, and the final costs to the funeral home and cemetery. Jeske was a very thorough, methodically minded man who didn't like to leave his work undone, yet there was very little left to do. The money he'd obtained from selling the large diamond ring Hazel gave him was nearly gone and he was forced to petition the estate to reimburse him for the money spent on bills and other expenses amounting to $59.90. It wasn't a very large amount to ask for, but Jeske truly needed the cash if he was going to make it through this nightmare. He tidied up the apartments at North Hayworth and moved to a duplex not far away on North Formosa Avenue. The home was owned by Clinton and Flo Lyle, dear friends of Jeske's former employers Lon and Hazel Chaney. The couple was well acquainted with all the heartbreaking details of the past few years and wanted to help Jeske any way they could. The Lyles lived on one side of the duplex and Jeske moved into the vacant side. The homes had a connecting door and shared a single telephone. Jeske was thankful for the Lyle's kindness, but the arrangement was meant to be a temporary one. For all the setbacks he encountered, Jeske never gave up hope that he would one day have a normal life with the woman he loved—Elaine Beuter.

Chapter 4:

A CHANCE FOR HAPPINESS TURNS TO DUST[1]

Nineteen-thirty-four ominously began with one of the worst floods to ever hit the Los Angeles Basin. Within a twenty-four hour period, over seven inches of rain fell on the area causing the ground to give way high up on the San Gabriel Mountains. The cascading water and earth destroyed at least two hundred homes and flooded over eight hundred more with mud and debris. Forty were confirmed dead, but that number and more would never be accounted for even after massive efforts were made to locate the dead and injured. It was a very somber and sobering way to start the New Year. The polio epidemic, labor unrest, and increasing violence throughout Los Angeles and the rest of the country fueled the already-tense atmosphere.

Somehow, through all of the turmoil, Jeske made the big decision to ask Elaine to marry him. The wedding took place on Saturday, June 30th, far away from the prying eyes of Hollywood, in the town of Santa Ana—south of Los Angeles in Orange County. There were no friends or family present—only the minister and a couple of witnesses that were found at the courthouse. Elaine was flush with the thought of the inheritance Jeske had received—or that she *thought* he had received. It's all too easy to believe that in his rush of enthusiasm and excitement over the marriage, Jeske may have neglected to mention to Elaine that he didn't actually have all the money just yet. He may have sincerely believed the inheritance would be available to him any day, but the back and forth between the lawyers and the beneficiaries that had been going on—and continued to go on—should have told him differently. Jeske couldn't even bring himself to tell Elaine he no longer had the fabulous diamond ring Hazel gave him. One of these days, he thought, the truth would all come out and she would understand. At least he hoped she would. Plans were made to pack up the Ford coupe on July 14th and head off to the mountains of Big Pine to enjoy their honeymoon in the cabin Lon Chaney had built for him on the banks of Big Pine Creek. It was such a beautiful place to start their marriage and the world seemed very bright and hopeful to the two newlyweds. Before they left for Big Pine, they rented a new apartment at 4649 Beverly Boulevard. It was a very modest one-bedroom place on the fifth floor with a large picture-window overlooking what were then palm tree-lined streets in a residential district. The apartment was almost too small and probably was meant to serve as a stepping stone to the larger home Jeske felt he could afford after he received his inheritance. Elaine was not entirely thrilled by the no-frills apartment, but it would certainly do for now.

At her crowded home on Denker Avenue, Joy Parker sat in the living room with her husband Lynden, brother-in-law, Oliver Fricke, and her young hoodlum friends. Fricke routinely "fenced" stolen goods, which made him a welcome ally to the Parkers and their "gang." The older couple got a big kick out of riding around town with Britton, Dorsey, and Russell scouting out possible "hits." So far, the action had been very small time. As July rolled around, the "boys" became increasingly willing to take bigger risks if the stakes were high enough. They started off by pulling several daring robberies by jumping on the running boards of vehicles stopped at a stop sign on a lonely side street. There was even a count of rape lodged against the boys when one young victim—a 20-year-old girl—told of how she was taken to a remote area in the hills and raped by three men. The take was minimal, but the thrills were big enough to satisfy the jaded group. The newspapers took the bait and ran sensational stories of this ruthless "kidnapping gang." There were others involved—associates of Britton and Dorsey—and the crime spree was widening daily. Russell had some remnants of a conscience left in him, though, and he was losing interest in the game. He kept his feelings to himself for now, yet looked for a way out.

It was during one of the warm nights of a Southern California summer when Britton, Russell, Dorsey and Ida Mae jumped in

Britton's tan Auburn Phaeton sedan and drove off to pick up the Parker's at their house. They were in the mood to hang out and drink and see what the evening would bring. Dorsey suggested they go down to Venice Pier and fool around at the amusement park at Ocean Beach. Lynden was a little reluctant to go, being more of a homebody, but Joy was excited about trying out the flight simulator plane they recently installed at the park. The Parker's said goodnight to the girls and they got in the car and headed south towards Venice. They went by way of the winding mountain two-lane highway through the homes and businesses tucked here and there around every turn. It was a beautiful evening for fun on the beach, and the amusement park was crowded with people looking for a good time. The gang walked around a bit and played a few games—Joy got her chance on the plane simulator—and after an hour or so they decided to head back home. The younger guys laughed at Joy and picked on her in the car about how they had bribed one of the ride operators to stop the ride up in the air while Joy was in the car to scare her. It worked, all right, and they laughed until they were hoarse about the horrified expression she had on her face. The group decided to stop at the Old Heidelberg Beer Garden and get something to eat and a few glasses of beer and wine. While sitting there listening to the all-girl orchestra, Britton, Russell, Dorsey and the Parkers began developing a plan for a series of robberies. Joy was drinking quite a bit and started rambling on about someone she wanted to get even with—settle a score. She knew Britton had just overhauled the Auburn's engine, and asked him if he'd like to "put some mileage" on it—kind of test it out. Deep down, Joy had felt slighted by the fact Hazel did not remember her in her will. She thought for certain she would receive something for all the attention she paid to Cora Chaney and Hazel during those final days. That should have counted for something. When no inheritance was forthcoming, Joy became bitter and her thoughts focused on the one person she felt received what was rightfully hers—John Jeske. With their family connection and now a bond of hatred for Jeske, it's easy to believe Joy Parker and Creighton Chaney knew each other well and spoke of their pain and humiliation. It stung even more deeply when Joy saw Jeske with a new car and lots of cash in his pocket. He's way too "flashy," she thought. All that was left to Joy now was revenge and a chance to recover something from Hazel's estate from Jeske. The young thugs listened to Joy intently and began to formulate their plans to bag all that wonderful loot. They finished their drinks and headed back towards Los Angeles. On the way, Joy told them Jeske had a huge diamond ring valued at $8,000, and lots of sterling silver items, such as matching picture frames and silverware. There was much more cash, too—almost a quarter of a million dollars. With every passing minute, Joy's inebriated brain inflated Jeske's net worth higher and higher until he seemed like a multi-millionaire walking around with thousand dollar bills in his pocket. She boasted that she had a connection at the movie studio who could move a large diamond like the one Jeske had and give her cold, hard cash with no questions asked. There had been a large amount of alcohol consumed by all that night, and the idea of robbing Jeske of his inheritance seemed more and more plausible. It wasn't long before the Auburn was cruising down the streets of West Hollywood looking for the place on North Formosa where Joy said Jeske had been living.

Joy had a plan to lure Jeske right where they wanted him so they could rough him up and take the money and expensive trinkets they were sure he had in his possession. Originally, Ida Mae was going to go up to Jeske's door and see if he'd answer when she knocked. If he opened the door, Ida was to give him a story about being a young actress who had to go out on location early that morning and she needed his help with her make-up. The fact was well known that Jeske had been a make-up assistant, so there's a chance he would have let Ida in. The plan backfired, though, when Jeske did not come to the door. Ida Mae got back in the sedan and they headed around the corner to an all-night drug store on Western Avenue. It was nearly 3 a.m. by this time, but it didn't matter. The plan was to have Ida Mae—who sounded innocent enough—call Jeske and give him the story about the actress needing make-up help. Joy felt sure Jeske would take the bait and go wherever they told him to, or at least agree to open his door in the wee hours to this "actress" in need of his services. Joy had Jeske's phone number—Gladstone 7537—and gave it to Ida Mae to make the call. Joy loitered nearby, pretending to play pinball and listening to every word. Ida dialed the number, but heard a woman's voice on the other line. She had gotten Mrs. Lyle out of bed and she wasn't especially happy about it. Ida Mae asked to speak to Mr. Jeske and was told he wasn't there.

"Well, this is very important," the flustered young woman said, "Would you please connect me with his apartment?"

Mrs. Lyle was feeling a little perturbed and answered shortly, "Mr. Jeske is not here!"

Jeske had moved out not long ago to the new apartment on Beverly Boulevard with his wife Elaine and gave Mrs. Lyle his new number in case he received any calls. She gave Ida Mae the number and tried to go back to sleep. Ida Mae hung up the phone and walked back to the sedan. Joy was already there and looking annoyed at the girl. She gave the details of her conversation and before long Joy told Ida Mae to get back in there and try again. Ida Mae reluctantly went back into the drug store and called the number Mrs. Lyle had given her. There was no answer. She tried two more times, but still there was nothing. Desperate now not to fail, Ida Mae rang Mrs. Lyle back.

Angry at being disturbed once again, Mrs. Lyle shouted "Do you know what time it is, young woman?"

Ida timidly answered, "Yes, I know it is very late, but I must get hold of him before morning."

Mrs. Lyle had had enough and angrily snapped "Well, I don't give a darn and don't ring this number again!"

The line abruptly disconnected in Ida Mae's ear.

The worried girl went back again to the car and told the gang what had happened. Joy was not overly concerned by this failed attempt to reach Jeske. She knew if he didn't have weekend business in town, Jeske would most likely be at his cabin in Big Pine. They went back to the house on Denker Avenue to pick up a few things for the trip. Britton and Dorsey put a leather bag and a package wrapped in newspaper into the trunk. Russell was feeling a bit lethargic from the alcohol and lack of sleep, and wasn't paying much attention to what his two friends were up to. While their backs were turned, curiosity got the best of Russell and he went over to the trunk to check out the bags. He found two guns—a .44 automatic revolver and a .32—a change of clothes, some rags, and a bundle of rope. Russell quickly put the items back where he found them and settled into the back seat. With Lynden and Joy Parker and Ida Mae in the front seat and the young men in back, the gang drove off to put some gas in the car before making the long drive up to the Sierra Nevada Mountains.

The motley group made their way in the big, lumbering sedan through the winding gravel highways toward the mountains. They had to stop a few times for gas, food, and to make repairs. The Auburn started acting up, so the boys took off the carburetor, cleaned it up and repacked the vacuum tank. Britton cursed the mechanic who had overhauled his sedan only recently, and did his best with Russell's help to get the car on the road again. They were able to finally make it to Big Pine, but the engine lacked compression and wasn't able to get the heavy machine and its cargo over the steep incline which led down to the cabins just outside of town. Britton and Russell got out and made one last attempt to fix the vacuum tank problem. Ida was sleepy, so she stayed in the back seat while the Parker's got out and walked down to the small creek. The couple took their shoes and stockings off and waded in the clear, cool water. The scenery couldn't have been more beautiful, with the tall pines and early morning sounds of the creek gurgling and the birds and squirrels busy in the trees overhead. Ironic, considering the purpose for this little joy ride. The boys struck out on getting the machine to pull them over the little hill, so they were forced to take the car into the one garage in town to see if the mechanic there could fix them up. Joy was feeling a little queasy from the effects of the winding roads and the large amount of alcohol she had consumed the evening before, and she decided to stay with the car at the garage. The others went on to a local café to get some breakfast. Ida Mae promised to bring back an ice cream cone for Joy.

The mechanic—a man named Smith—chatted a little with Joy and then got to work under the hood trying to locate the problem. A local man, Russell Stewart, and a friend of Smith's came in to shoot the breeze and see who the strangers were. Stewart and Smith talked a little about a mix-up that had happened with a car battery belonging to a mutual acquaintance of theirs—John Jeske. Joy's ears perked up at the mention of "Jeske," and she asked if that was the same Jeske who had been Lon Chaney's chauffeur. With that, Smith and Stewart started opening up a little about the Chaneys. Smith asked Joy if she knew Mrs. Chaney had died. Joy acted very sorrowful and told the men she knew all about it. Smith looked down and shook his head saying, "It is too bad, because she was a wonderful little woman." Joy quickly agreed and added, "Cancer is a horrible death." The men were a bit taken aback when Joy continued on to say that Hazel had died of the same thing Lon passed away from, and it wouldn't surprise her if Jeske died the same way. She stopped talking at this point and didn't offer an explanation for her cryptic prophecy. Stewart then dropped the bombshell that Jeske was there in Big Pine with his wife. Joy was noticeably startled saying she couldn't believe he would have married so soon. Smith smiled broadly and nodded his head adding, "Yeah, he married a blonde!" Joy managed to mutter something about how Jeske was keeping his marriage a secret and "they would have a nice time when they got back to Los Angeles." It didn't take long for Smith to fix the Auburn's carburetor problem, and the gang piled in the vehicle and headed down the road toward Glacier Lodge. Stewart told Joy where to find Jeske's cabin—he had actually been the one who built the cabin for Jeske, so he knew it well.

Over at Glacier Lodge, Eunice Chapman, who managed the Lodge with her husband, was going about her duties when a large woman accompanied by two men came through the front door. Normally, Mr. Chapman would be there to greet visitors, but he had had a long night and was sleeping-in this particular afternoon. It was mid-afternoon now, and the woman—Joy Parker—told Mrs. Chapman she was interested in renting one of the cabins. There were three available, and Joy was first shown one, not far from the Lodge. Mrs. Chapman noticed immediately the woman really wasn't interested in the size of the cabin or its amenities, but that she kept looking out the window. Finally, Joy asked Mrs. Chapman if you could see the "Chaney" cabin from there. They went out on the porch and Mrs. Chapman realized it wasn't possible, and said "No, we can't see it on account of the trees." At the second cabin, Joy asked the same question and this time Mrs. Chapman asked if she meant the Chaney cabin or the one he built for Jeske. Joy felt a little nervous now, but confirmed it was the Jeske cabin she was interested in. No matter, though. None of the cabins had a clear view of Jeske's place. They would have to think of some other way to survey the area to locate Jeske.

The fact Jeske was now a married man complicated things quite a bit. They would have to regroup and figure out another way to get the goods from Jeske. A plan was quickly devised by Britton, who took over as the leader of this hapless gang, and they drove the Auburn on the narrow road that went directly past the cabin where Jeske and his wife were staying. As they got close to the cabin, they saw a couple walking on the road just in front of the place. Joy pointed in their direction and said, "That's John, but don't let him see us!" She quickly put a handkerchief up to hide her face and Lynden scrunched down in the seat. They couldn't risk being identified by Jeske or all bets would be off. Jeske and Elaine had been out enjoying a short hike along the trails. Elaine, dressed in white corduroy pants, white blouse, and white shoes seemed somewhat out of place on the dusty dirt trails, but this Hollywood blonde needed to be fashionable at all times. Having had more experience in the back country with Chaney, Jeske knew to wear something more rugged and donned a pair of overalls, a casual shirt, and some boots. There had been a little friction between them this afternoon, and Jeske was ready for an especially frosty evening.

The Auburn sedan drove by the cabin once again and stopped near the end of the road. Britton got out of the car and brusquely ordered a sleepy Dorsey to get out as well. Dorsey rubbed his eyes and stirred a bit, but he moved too slowly. Britton angrily yelled "Get out of the car!" and moved toward the back to retrieve his leather bag and newspaper wrapped package. Dorsey got out and Russell slipped in behind the wheel with the Parker's in front and Ida Mae still in the backseat. She'd been too sleepy and too afraid of Britton to say or do very much on this trip. She had learned it was best to play along and not arouse Britton's anger in any way. It wasn't healthy for her. Britton gave Russell detailed instructions to drive south back to Los Angeles, drop off the Parker's, and then turn around and drive back up towards Independence, stopping just outside of Saugus. Britton and Dorsey would rob Jeske and meet up with Russell and Ida Mae there. No one actually said how the boys would drive down to Saugus, but at least Ida Mae knew that whatever Britton set his mind to, he usually did it no matter what. This time would be no different. Russell dutifully did his part and drove out of Big Pine down the bumpy gravel highway to Los Angeles. Before they left, Joy Parker had warned Britton to be careful of Jeske—he was "rather tricky." Britton wasn't worried. With two revolvers pointed at his face it would unlikely that Jeske would give them much trouble. They were also capable of torture, like the time they put cigarette ashes on a man's eyelids, or took a poor old man's shoes off and stomped on his toes.

At around 8:30 p.m., the Jeske cabin was already quiet and settling in for the night. The friction between Jeske and his new bride was still a bit raw, but they had patched up their differences. Still, Elaine said she had a headache and went to bed early. Jeske stayed up a bit longer, but was now readying himself for bed. He was startled by a knock on the screen door. Jeske opened the door, but left the screen door locked for the time being. There were two young men standing there he had never seen before.

"We have a package for you from Mr. Chapman," said the blond-haired one holding a newspaper wrapped package on his arm.

"Oh, fine," said Jeske and unlocked the screen door.

Britton quickly removed the package from his arm to reveal a large revolver that he pressed in towards Jeske's stomach. Britton and Dorsey pushed Jeske backwards into the cabin and ordered the frightened man to lie face down on the ground. While Britton bound and gagged Jeske with the bits of material and rope contained in the package, Dorsey searched the cabin. He found Elaine sleeping in her bed and quietly went over to one side. He pressed the gun to her cheek, startling her awake.

"Keep quiet and you won't get hurt," Dorsey said.

Elaine sat up and asked if she could go over to the closet to get her dressing gown and slippers as she was clad only in her pajamas. Dorsey didn't see the harm in it, so he allowed her to get her things and then marched her out into the living room. Elaine was told to lie down next to her husband and was also bound and gagged. Before long, Elaine started choking and her gag was removed. She asked if she could have a drink of water, and Dorsey went with her to the kitchen. Elaine was very adept at sizing up a man and playing to his instincts, whatever they may be. Jerry—that's what she learned Dorsey was called—wasn't such a bad guy, she thought. He might prove useful. She looked out of the kitchen doorway and saw Jeske lying there with his face to the carpet and trussed up like an animal. Britton's voice was getting more and more angry with each attempt to question Jeske about the whereabouts of that $8,000 Chaney diamond ring, the securities and bonds Jeske was supposed to have inherited, and that huge pile of cash. What he was hearing just didn't add up.

Jeske pleaded with him—through the gag in his mouth—that he didn't have the diamond; he sold it long time ago at Brock Jewelers in Los Angeles for $1,800. He had no other money from the estate, as it hadn't gone through probate yet. Elaine pleaded with Dorsey to take off her husband's gag. Dorsey nodded in Jeske's direction and said easily, "You can do it." She quickly went over and took off the gag and loosened the rope around Jeske's hands. He still had on his blindfold. They couldn't risk being identified, though it didn't seem to matter to them that Elaine could see them very clearly. As Jeske sat up, Dorsey came over and rifled through his pockets to find that fat wad of bills Joy said he always had on him. No bills; no diamond, only four, one dollar bills and a pocket watch.[2] Jeske pleaded with the thugs to let him keep the watch, as it had been a present to him and was of great sentimental value. He said if it was worth one dollar to them it would be worth more than a thousand dollars to Jeske. Britton mockingly said, "How much is it worth to you now?" Jeske was mentally very quick, and saw an opportunity to get the watch back for very little. He said it would be worth $50 to him to get it back. Britton thought about it for a few seconds and then said, "Well, when you get back in town, carry around fifty dollars, and some day someone will drive by you and wave that watch in front of you. Give him fifty dollars and you get your watch back." Jeske agreed to the terms.

Britton had had enough with Jeske and what he believed to be lies about the diamond and all the money and he intended to make him talk. He shoved the barrel of his gun up to Jeske's mouth and rubbed it back and forth across his teeth. Though incredibly frightened, Jeske continued to insist he had sold the diamond and purchased bonds with the proceeds. He had no ready cash to give them. Dorsey had found Jeske's bank book in a suitcase and showed Britton the balance: $91. So *this* was the multi-millionaire, flashy, pocket full of bills guy that Joy Parker told them about? If this wasn't such a life-and-death serious situation, Britton and Dorsey would have broken out laughing. The joke was on them, though, but not for long.

Desperate not to go back to Los Angeles empty handed, Britton told Jeske to write a check made out to "cash" for $76. He thought a round number picked at random wouldn't spark as much undue attention. Jeske complied with the request and gave them the check to hold until it could be cashed. Britton and Dorsey made one last inspection of the cabin, ransacking and ripping apart anything that looked like a likely hiding place for valuables of any kind. All they found was a .22 gauge high-powered rifle, a shotgun, and a .32 caliber pistol. They took the guns, the Jeske's suitcases and a leather jacket belonging to Elaine, as well as a small mattress. After the nearly four-hour ordeal was over, the Jeske's were taken outside to the Ford coupe that was parked in the driveway. Britton wanted the Jeske's to ride in the rumble seat all the way back to Los Angeles, but Elaine turned on her charm once again and pleaded with Dorsey to allow them to ride up front. She said promised to act right and not say a word. Dorsey's heart was touched, and he asked Britton if it was OK for the couple to sit inside with them. Britton reluctantly agreed and the suitcases and the other booty was piled into the rumble seat instead. Dorsey got in the driver's seat with Jeske in the middle and Britton on the passenger side. Elaine sat on her husband's lap.[3] It was a very cramped and uncomfortable ride on those rough, bumpy roads leading down from the mountain towards Los Angeles.

It was after 11:30 p.m. and all the shops were closed up tight. Jeske had said his friend at the gas station in Big Pine would probably cash the check for him, but no one was there when they drove up. Britton said they would have to drive all the way back to Los Angeles, then, so Jeske could cash the check. Jeske was overwrought with dread by this revelation, but he remained stoic and determined to survive this latest test. The Ford needed some gas, so they pulled into Lone Pine. Near the gas station was an old dance hall type of eatery called the "Spanish Inn." The boys were hungry, and Elaine said she needed to use the ladies room. It was agreed that they would go in and get some food and then hit the road for Los Angeles. Inside the rather tired looking building was a large dance floor with tables and booths along the perimeter. A jukebox and some slot machines were arranged on one end to amuse those who didn't quite feel like dancing. By this time, the place was nearly empty and getting ready to close down, so the couples slipped in without much notice. The waitress turned on the main lights and sat the group down in a booth in a dimly lit corner—Dorsey next to Elaine and Britton close by Jeske. All the while, Britton had his revolver pressed into Jeske's side so he knew not to make a fuss or try to get away. Jeske was feeling sick from the rag that had been thrust down his throat, and was not at all hungry. He thought that maybe he could keep down a cup of coffee to help him stay alert. Elaine didn't seem quite as fazed by the whole, horrible situation, and asked for a glass of wine and some cigarettes. Somehow she was resigned to whatever fate had in store for them and seemed to be trying to make the best of things. After a short while, Britton gave Jeske a shove and ordered him back out to the car. Elaine asked Dorsey for a little money to play the slots and he thought that sounded like a fun idea. Jeske sat in the Ford for what seemed like an eternity with Britton's gun at his side as he waited for his wife to finish playing the slot machine with one of her kidnappers. It was beginning to seem all too surreal at this point, yet the cold metal of Britton's gun in his side brought him quickly back to reality. Finally, Elaine came out, cheerfully announcing that she had won some money at the machine. She split her winnings with Dorsey and they slid in the coupe to begin their journey once again.

There was one more stop for gas near Mojave, then straight on to about three miles outside of Saugus. As they drove nearer to the spot Britton had instructed to Russell to wait, they could clearly see the big Auburn sedan parked by the side of the road in the early morning light. Britton drove the Ford up next to his machine and threw a coat over Jeske's head as he pushed him out of the car. Dorsey also got out and took his seat in the back of the Auburn. Ida Mae slipped next to Elaine inside the Ford and waited for Britton to finish giving more instructions to Russell and Dorsey. They were all going to drive back to their rented house on Leota Street and park the vehicles in the garage out back. Russell, Dorsey, and Jeske took off in the Auburn, while Britton, Elaine and Ida Mae headed out in Jeske's Ford coupe.

The smooth V8 of the brand new Ford hummed with the kind of power Britton's bigger 12-cylinder engine couldn't hope to match. He was impressed with the machine, but he was more preoccupied with what he would tell Joy and Lynden when they got back to Los Angeles, and more importantly, how to bring up the fact he felt he had been double-crossed. All he knew was that he wasn't going to be left holding the bag on this botched Jeske job. It was close to 5 a.m. when the group made it to the dingy garage in back of the Parker's rented house. They put the vehicles inside and locked the doors. It had been a long drive, and Britton was worn out. He unpacked the mattress they had brought back from the cabin in Big Pine and took it into the empty house to lie down for a while and take a nap. Ida Mae dutifully went with him. Jeske was roughly moved to his Ford and was able to see Elaine for the first time since they left Lone Pine. Dorsey and Russell sat on either side of the vehicle and started to talk loudly about all the crimes they had committed and the tortures they'd performed. Russell laughed as he mentioned the guy he bent a finger back on. Boy, did he give up the goods after that! The not-so-subtle bragging was all designed to intimidate the Jeske's and keep them in constant fear so they would remain obedient. It worked—the couple was too terrified to even move, let alone try to make an escape.

About 10 a.m., Britton came out of the house along with Ida Mae and went over to the Ford coupe. He gave his young girlfriend a .44 automatic to use to move Elaine over to the Auburn. The gun was huge in the small woman's hand and she could barely manage it, though she kept her best "tough girl" mask on so as not to let on to her captive that she wished she could be far away from this place. Elaine was perceptive enough to see worry in the young girl's face and her own wedding ring on her finger. Ida Mae desperately wanted to pretend she was really married to Britton—didn't they tell everyone they were married? It was only a matter of time, or at least that's what he told her. Ida Mae noticed Elaine's piercing gaze and was convicted by it. She tried to shake it off by saying, "You won't recognize me because I'm a stranger." Elaine just softly said, "I'm not trying to recognize you. I'm just surprised at such a young girl holding that awful gun." Ida Mae didn't quite know how to answer that, so just continued to point the gun at Elaine and hope it would all be over soon.

Britton and Jeske drove off in the Ford coupe up to Hollywood to the Bank of America on the corner of Hollywood and Highland to cash the check Jeske had been forced to write while a prisoner at the cabin in Big Pine. Jeske was instructed to drop Britton off about a block away and proceed directly to the bank—no funny stuff. "Remember, we have your wife," Britton snarled as he got out of the car. Jeske knew he had to comply or face the possibility of his wife being harmed, or even killed. He nervously walked into the bank, searching the faces of all who were waiting in the lobby. Britton hinted some of the "gang" may be there watching him as a safeguard against any heroics on Jeske's part. Jeske went up to the teller and presented the check. With his $76 in hand, he hurriedly walked out of the bank and back into his Ford. His instructions were to drive around the block until he spotted Britton. After a couple times around the block, Britton appeared on the corner and was picked up by Jeske. Jeske handed over the money and was told to drive up Highland over the Tujunga Pass to an isolated, sparsely populated area appropriately named Dark Canyon Road. Britton ordered Jeske to park the car and wait. His wife would soon be with him. It seemed like he had been sitting there forever when he finally saw Elaine coming around the corner on foot. Russell and Dorsey had driven her up to the canyon in the Auburn not long after Britton and Jeske headed off for the bank. Elaine made it to the Ford and gave her husband the keys. Their relief was unimaginable, though the ordeal wasn't quite over yet.

The Jeske's went home to their cozy apartment on Beverly Boulevard, showered, and changed clothes. Jeske was still too sick to eat any solid food. The combination of the abject terror and the rag that had been stuffed down his throat made him unable to eat normally, but he tried to get by on soup and other liquids. Elaine was put off by the rough treatment, but otherwise seemed strangely nonplussed. She was more concerned about the fact Jeske never told her about the expensive diamond Hazel Chaney gave him, or anything else about his inheritance—especially the part about not being able to get his hands on the money for a long, long time. For now, she would keep these troubling thoughts mainly to herself, but at the first opportunity she was determined to have it out with her new husband.

Jeske phoned his lawyer friend, Ralph W. Smith, and told him all about the kidnapping and robbery and asked for advice. A strange thing to do, in retrospect, considering it was a heinous crime that needed to be punished. Why wonder whether or not to call the authorities, or what the ramifications would be? The problem was rooted in the very effective psychological warfare the young thugs had employed with their unfortunate victims. Britton, especially, was good at making it sound like there was an entire legion of gang members at his beck and call who were ready to make the Jeske's life miserable if they even so much as thought about calling the police. Britton told them their every move would be watched by one of these nameless gangsters, so the couple had better stay put in their apartment until they get a phone call about making a swap for the pocket watch and Elaine's wedding ring. Smith advised Jeske to keep quiet about the whole affair until they heard from the kidnappers again. This sounded easy enough on the surface, but it meant hours and days spent in agonizing suspense waiting for the phone to ring, afraid to go out for groceries or anything at all. Jeske agreed to do as his friend suggested, though, and tried to go about life with Elaine as normal. Nothing would ever be "normal" again between Jeske and his new wife.

In the meantime, Britton and the Parker's discussed the Jeske situation over breakfast the day after the Jeske's were released. Joy Parker was livid. Where was the diamond? Where were the sterling silver items? What happened to the wads of cash? Britton explained the whole thing to Joy, but conveniently left out the part about the $76.00 check, or the swap being planned for the watch and ring. He did tell her about the guns and the suitcases, along with miscellaneous items taken from the cabin. All small change, though. Joy could do nothing but accept Britton's story—as lame as she thought it was—and was reduced to fuming, "Next time I'll have to check into things myself!" Later that day the guns were brought out and Lynden took one of Jeske's suits. He was the only one small enough to fit Jeske's clothes, and he liked the sleek styling of the expensive suit. Joy fancied the .22 high-power rifle, which accidentally went off when Britton was displaying it, just missing Russell's head. Play time was over.

Several days passed for the Jeske's before that phone call finally came. The voice on the other line said it was a "Mr. Williams" and he asked if Jeske had the fifty bucks he was supposed to give for the watch and ring. Whether he couldn't scrape it up in the week's time he had been waiting, or it was a ploy to stall for a chance to contact the authorities, Jeske anxiously said he didn't have that kind of money on him, but could get it within a few days. "Mr. Williams" angrily said he'd call back on Thursday and slammed the receiver down. Jeske picked up the phone again and dialed the sheriff's office. Eugene W. Biscailuz, the flamboyant, and extremely popular, sheriff of Los Angeles County was known by many as the "Spanish Don." The diminutive, cigar-smoking Los Angeles native enjoyed being in the spotlight, and unabashedly participated in local rodeos and parades dressed in his finest riding clothes inspired by his Spanish heritage. 1934 was an election year, and Biscailuz was continuing his tough fight on the wave of crime that had infected his beloved city. With the help of the District Attorney, Buron Fitts, and Deputy D.A. Robert P. Stewart, Biscailuz organized what he called "welcoming committees" at the county line to make sure any known undesirables didn't make it into his territory. Biscailuz was extremely proud to point out the fact that no kidnapping committed within Los Angeles County has gone unsolved or unprosecuted. Biscailuz and his department always got their man.

The sheriff himself wanted to handle the Jeske case. Another kidnapping in his jurisdiction could potentially become a thorn in his side and hurt his chances for re-election in November. He wanted to personally ensure that this case was taken care of swiftly and decisively. Jeske told the story to Biscailuz and about the plan to swap the watch and ring for the money. A plan was put into place by the seasoned sheriff to entrap the kidnapper and take down the entire gang. Jeske would go to the planned meeting place on July 27th a little after 8 p.m. with the money, but he wouldn't be alone. Sheriff's deputies, deputies from the District Attorney's office, and an undercover F.B.I. agent were all on hand to "welcome" the worthless scum who would arrive to shake down Jeske. The plan went off without a hitch. Ida Mae rode with Britton for a ways on the streetcar, but got off at 9th and Broadway and headed back home. Britton came alone on foot to the pedestrian zone for the streetcars at the corner of Tenth and Hill where Jeske was waiting for him. As soon as he saw Jeske's car, he jumped on the running boards and reached in for the latch to open the door. He was almost inside to grab the money Jeske was holding out to him, when a sheriff's deputy came up from behind and told him he was under arrest. Britton had counted too much on his intimidation job on Jeske. The jig was up, and he knew it. The only thing Britton could do now was to try to find a way to dig out of the big hole he'd dug for himself. He wasn't going down for this alone.

Britton was first taken to the D.A.'s office near the crime scene and then transferred to the sheriff's office. There, he made a full confession giving up the names of all of his playmates—including his girlfriend, Ida Mae. They were quickly rounded up and brought to the station and placed in their holding cells. The Jeskes came down too to give their statements and retrieve some of their personal belongings that the deputies were able to recover from the thugs during the arrests. Lynden and Joy Parker pretended to not know what in the world they were being arrested for and tried to look as innocent as possible. As fate would have it, Jeske and Elaine bumped into Joy in the hallway on their way to pick up their stolen belongings. Joy played it cool and asked Jeske, "What are you doing here?" Jeske, at this point completely unaware of the Parker's involvement in the kidnapping, casually answered back, "What are *you* doing here? I'm kind of surprised to see you here." Joy had to go, so they simply shook hands and parted ways. Jeske had forgotten to introduce his new bride to Lon's cousin, but it didn't seem to matter at the time. The deputy escorting Joy down the hall saw the interaction between Parker and Jeske and couldn't help asking the large woman as he was helping her into the holding tank, "You don't like Mr. Jeske?" Joy's demeanor darkened considerably, perhaps reliving some past offense in her mind, as she hissed back, "I don't like him and never did."

Rounded up in the sting with the Jeske kidnappers were various thugs associated with Britton, Russell and Dorsey who had all been a party to various petty and not so petty crimes committed over a two-month period in the Los Angeles area. From stealing a truck full of eggs to an attempted rape—these boys were definitely emulating their gangster heroes. Ironically, one of the most notorious gangsters of that era—John Dillinger—was finally located and gunned down outside of a movie theater in Chicago on July 22, 1934. The news coverage of this event was overwhelming and even a week later was still dominating the front pages of newspapers across the country. The news of the Jeske kidnapping broke nationwide on Saturday, July 28th, and revealed to the world the horrific details of the Jeske's kidnapping, torture, and robbery. The Associated Press wire again made the claim that Jeske was Lon Chaney's make-up man: "John Jeske, the man responsible for the terrifying faces portrayed on the screen by the late Lon Chaney. . . ."⁴ The reporters who covered the crime locally soft-pedaled this description by simply saying Jeske had been Lon Chaney's long-time chauffeur and companion. The spotlight was once again on Jeske and he was not comfortable with all the attention. He avoided the press and refused to give any interviews. The quotes printed in the newspapers attributed to Jeske were taken from his statement given to the sheriff's office, which Sheriff Biscailuz was only too happy to release to the press. More positive publicity for his department was always good for business.

The publicity given to Jeske and the kidnapping infuriated Creighton Chaney. By this time he had appeared in quite a few movies—mostly Westerns—in bit roles. The pressure from RKO was increasing for Creighton to change his name to "Lon Chaney, Jr." This would increase his box office appeal and make him a much more lucrative package for the studio—it didn't matter what sort of acting ability he had. He was frustrated and sick of the day-to-day grind that never seemed to get him anywhere. His marriage was in name only and his drinking increased. Creighton was romantically involved with a photographer's model named Patsy Beck, and he made no secret of the affair. There were others too, and Dorothy Chaney knew the marriage was doomed. In this maelstrom of depression, Creighton once again flew into a rage when he saw Jeske referred to as his father's "make-up man." He contacted the *Los Angeles Times* and gave a heated statement to reporter Read Kendall, whose column, "Around and About in Hollywood," exposed the intimate details of celebrity lives. Creighton told Kendall Jeske was never employed as his father's make-up man, and in fact, "his father never was aided by anybody—except by a butler who helped him dress—when he prepared himself for his screen roles . . . Further, Chaney never used a stand-in or a double and performed all hazardous feats in his pictures in person." Creighton went on to say, "I am making this statement at such a late date because I am sick and tired of people trying to cash in on my father's fame when it is not due them." The son's anger is understandable, but very misplaced. It is painfully obvious that he was not really a confidant in the matter of his father's professional life, nor did he ever spend a great deal of time at the studio watching him at work. The details of the help that Chaney received in the areas of make-up and stunt work were printed in the newspapers in connection with some of the great actor's more dangerous and ambitions productions, namely, *The Hunchback of Notre Dame*. And who did Creighton think was his father's "butler"? The elder Chaney adamantly denied he ever had a valet or anything of that sort (which wasn't entirely true), so Creighton's statement about a "butler" is astounding. Either the son was so hurt and angry that he fabricated events in his father's life to reflect the skewed version of reality he wanted to believe in, or he blatantly lied to cover up the details he felt ashamed of for some reason. There is an inherent tragedy and sadness surrounding the way Creighton felt about his father and his own life, and he seemed to grasp at whatever means he could find to bolster his own fragile self-image. There had been others claiming to be Chaney's make-up man—make-up artist Leslie H. Carter, for one. Another make-up "expert," V.E. Meadows, was described in print as being "make-up man for the versatile Lon Chaney."[5] Creighton no doubt singled out Jeske to vent his wrath for all the injustices he felt were being perpetrated in his late father's name. Jeske would be on Creighton's radar screen for the rest of his life.

The Grand Jury convened on August 1, 1934 and swiftly charged Britton, Dorsey, Russell, Ida Mae, and the Parkers with multiple counts of kidnapping and robbery. The entire inquiry only lasted two days, and the formal trial was scheduled to begin on September

11th. The Jeske's needed to get away from all the scrutiny and pressure of Hollywood, and try to resume the honeymoon that had been so rudely interrupted. They got in the Ford coupe on August 16th and headed back up to Big Pine—to their peaceful mountain cabin. They were minor celebrities now, as word of the kidnapping had reached even the isolated communities in the surrounding areas. The Jeskes tried to blend in and relax, but John was constantly looking over his shoulder—expecting a thug to be lurking behind every bush. Elaine was annoyed at his nervous behavior and wanted to just loosen up and have some fun.

Evenings in the Glacier Lodge area of Big Pine were quiet, non-complicated affairs. The main source of entertainment for the locals was to gather at the Glacier Pack Train Station to talk, play a little music, and maybe sing along. Jeske and Elaine made their way down the dirt road one evening to the station to enjoy the company of some of the other couples in town. It was a lively, playful group this particular evening, and there was a little too much wine flowing. A tipsy Elaine began to get rather loud and started flirting with a local boy, Rowland Harwood. Jeske's face felt hot as he watched his wife shamelessly throwing herself at the young man, who had only a week before been married to another local girl, Babe Rossi. Babe tugged at her new husband's arm and tried to get him to leave—she had had just about enough of this disgusting display. Rowland was enjoying the spectacle, but didn't want to make Babe any more upset than she already was. The young couple got up and left the station to make their way home. Jeske also grabbed Elaine's arm and jerked her out of there. How could she make such a fool of him in public? What was she thinking? Jeske had to face the fact that his wife had a serious problem with alcohol and didn't take their marriage quite as seriously as he did.

Towards the end of September, a very strange crime took place in the home of Hazel's sister, Eleanor Lechert. She told the police that she and her husband Paul only left the house for about fifteen minutes to go down to the market, and when they returned they discovered their home had been burglarized. What caught the officer's attention was that the thieves knew exactly to go to the couple's bathroom, pull back the carpet, and open the trap door. Within that short fifteen minute span of time the thief or thieves managed to get in the house, empty the secret hiding place, and be long gone by the time the couple returned. Obviously they had been casing the house for some time. The crime was too methodical and neat to have been a random act. These crooks knew the Lecherts and they also knew that Eleanor had just inherited some very expensive jewelry from her sister, Hazel Chaney. All in all, Eleanor claims to have lost over $12,000 worth of jewelry, including the diamond watch engraved with her sister's name on the reverse.[6] She was devastated by the loss. The person or persons responsible for the crime were never apprehended, which only added more fuel to the fire of Jeske's growing paranoia. Could these criminals be part of Britton's gang?

Back in Hollywood, the couple tried as best they could to adjust to their lives again. By October 5th, all of the individuals responsible for the Jeske kidnapping had been sentenced to the maximum term allowed—life without the possibility of parole. The court in Los Angeles County had made a pledge to crack way down on kidnappers and they used this trial to send a message to anyone considering this unholy method of making a living. All along, the Parkers had claimed their innocence. They said they were drunk the night of the kidnapping and didn't know what Britton and the others were up to. When they woke up, they were in Big Pine, and so on. It was all too fantastic. Britton, Dorsey, Russell, and Ida Mae all testified that the Parkers were heavily involved and Joy Parker was the ringleader. Their stories were consistent and damning. The material proof of the Parker's involvement was lacking, though, but the jury felt the preponderance of testimony to the fact the Parker's put their young friends up to the crime was enough for them to bring back guilty verdicts. Unfortunately, it wouldn't be enough to hold them in jail for very long.

Creighton was still in turmoil over his stalled movie career and failing marriage. By a strange coincidence, the younger Chaney decided to let off some steam by going up to Big Pine on November 23rd to do some pheasant and cottontail hunting. He enjoyed the outdoors and the thrill of the hunt. Was he up there merely to hunt animals? Did he think Jeske may be up there at his cabin? Jeske had other things on his mind right now, and needed to remain in Los Angeles to try and establish himself in some kind of business. His money was nearly gone and seeing that the bulk of his inheritance was a long way off, he had to do something to earn a living. He couldn't ask Elaine to get a job—that would be a sign of his inability to provide for her in the traditional sense.

Jeske was drawn to the mountains, and had found a number of years back a special place of refuge tucked away in the Santa Monica mountain range known as the Alturas Country Club and Hotel. It wasn't much more than a large, rambling ranch-style house and some barns and stables owned by a savvy old businessman named Edward Henderson. Jeske had first discovered the place when a small-time boxer named Mushy Callahan selected the Alturas as a place to train for an upcoming prize fight back with Sammy Baker in 1927. Jeske and Chaney kept tabs on local boxers, especially the long shots, and took notice of the Alturas. The place was difficult to get to with a steep, narrow dirt road to climb. The terrain proved too difficult for Callahan and his trainers to get their equipment up to the Club and they were forced to abandon their plans and set-up camp at the Main Street Gym.[7] During Prohibition, the Alturas was known to a handful of adventurous souls who were looking for illegal booze, gambling, and a place to hide out for a while. The plush restaurant and horse stables provided a façade of respectability to an otherwise-questionable enterprise. For Jeske, the Alturas seemed like a perfect place to provide a temporary escape from his troubles and, possibly, a stable business venture. Jeske had made the acquaintance of a man named James Doyle at the Alturas during one of his visits. Doyle was a janitor at the local veteran's home in nearby Sawtelle, and was looking for a way to make it on his own. The two men decided to pool their resources and approached Henderson with an offer to buy out the business end of the Alturas Hotel. The Bill of Sale was drawn up and filed on November 2, 1934. Jeske and his partner would obtain all the furnishings from the main hotel, the six guest rooms, the two rooms kept for the waiter and cook, and all the fixtures, including the kitchen appliances. The future seemed bright for Jeske, who unfortunately did not have any tangible experience running a business or the working capital to keep it going. Jeske and Doyle managed to come up with the $1,250 needed for the down payment, and Henderson helped the partners obtain a mortgage to pay off the $1,500.00 to complete the purchase. Jeske was banking—literally—on the big inheritance he would certainly get any day now. He had high hopes for his new business plan, despite Elaine's reservations. The Alturas would very soon become a cornerstone in the new drama unfolding in Jeske's pain-filled life.

Chapter 5:

A LIFE IN THE SHADOWS ONCE MORE

The hills above Los Angeles in the Brentwood Heights area were a beautiful, untamed, wooded retreat from the hustle and bustle of the city. The road connecting Sunset Boulevard in Beverly Hills with the main mountain highway to the ocean north of Santa Monica had only been completed as of 1926,[1] and though residential and business development had been steadily increasing along this new thoroughfare, the majority of land was still full of lush vegetation and tall trees by 1935. The Alturas Hotel and Country Club was tucked away up a steep, barely marked road off of North Kenter Avenue in the Kenter Canyon section of Brentwood Heights. A few residential developments had sprung up along Homewood Road, Tiger Tail, Rockingham to the west, and many other little curvy streets carving out more and more space on the mountainside.

When his wife Delia was alive, Edward Henderson owned a road house sort of establishment he and his wife operated out of their home on Bonhill Road, just across from Kenter Avenue. The "country club" itself was mainly a few stables with horses available to ride and a barn that could be used as a gym if properly equipped. After 1932, the year Delia passed away, Henderson moved his business to the larger ranch home on the grounds of the country club and continued his restaurant and inn, catering to the adventurous travelers motoring along the new boulevard, or more often couples looking for a discrete place to meet where none of their friends or family would recognize them. As long as they paid their bill and didn't break any furniture, Henderson turned a blind eye to behavior that may have been a little unsavory or illegal. His two employees—a waiter and a cook—were from Eastern Europe and Austria. The cook, a middle-aged woman named Bella Kowriak,[2] was born in the same region of Poland where Jeske was from. It is easy to see the three of them conversing in German and Polish about the families they left behind and the trouble their homelands had to endure.

The camaraderie Jeske may have found at the Alturas was a long way off by the time he pulled into the underground garage at the Dover Apartments in West Los Angeles. Elaine was drinking more and putting up with less. The tiny apartment was like a straight-jacket to her. Where was this carefree, exciting Hollywood life she had envisioned for the two of them? To make up for her frustration, Elaine looked up some old friends she had met at the studio, and others she had met at the local bars, and began to invite them up to the apartment at an increasingly frequent rate. She never bothered to ask her husband if it was OK with him—she just had them sit down on the couch and started the alcohol flowing. Jeske hated this spectacle night after night and found himself becoming disgusted by the very sight of his wife. She was loud and offensive at times, flirting with the male guests as if her husband wasn't even in the room. By the time she came to bed she reeked of booze and was barely coherent. He couldn't bear to touch her, let alone make love to her. During the day, Elaine's head pounded from the large amount of alcohol she consumed the night before and she screamed her demands at Jeske over the breakfast table. What could he do? When pushed into a corner Jeske turned inward and became a stone image whenever Elaine raised her voice to him. This only infuriated her more and she lashed out about everything that was wrong with their marriage and her life. By this time, though, Jeske was usually already out the door and walking down the five flights of steps to make his way to freedom. This situation was at the breaking point and could not stand the application of much more pressure.

Jeske had enough trouble of his own right now. His "dream" business—running the Alturas Hotel—was proving demanding and unmanageable for him. The money just wasn't there, and he needed lots of it if he hoped to meet all the daily demands of operating a restaurant and renting rooms. His so-called pal, James Doyle, was proving to be unreliable and Jeske quickly found himself holding the bag when it came time to make their mortgage payments. By

January 15th, Jeske had taken sole responsibility for the Alturas and would try to make the best of things on his own. Henderson was there for some support in running the business, but he wasn't willing to loan Jeske any more money. The stress Jeske was feeling was enormous and he had very few options left to him.

On the evening of February 25th, Jeske and his wife were settling in for a rare quiet evening at their apartment to relax and listen to the radio. As it neared 9:30 p.m., Jeske got up and turned the dial to search the channels for something of interest. There was a new drama series premiering on the Los Angeles based station KMTR that evening called *In the Crimelite*, produced and written by a veteran of Los Angeles radio, George Neff. For the premier show, Sheriff Eugene Biscailuz was to introduce the story of the kidnapping of John and Elaine Jeske in the summer of 1934. The couple sat in their living room in a state of shock as they heard the details of their horrible ordeal played out as a drama on the airwaves by a group of actors headed by Robert Horner and Virginia Howard. As one would expect, the details were twisted and sensationalized even more to increase the appeal to the radio audience. Somehow, Jeske came off as weak and powerless to help his suffering wife. The show was soon over, the radio turned off, but the negative effects of this night would linger. Elaine was furious and a heated argument broke out in what had been a peaceful apartment up until that moment. Jeske turned his back on the violent ranting of his wife and walked out the door without a word. She ran after him down the corridor and demanded to know where he was going, but she received no answer. Jeske got in his car and drove the fifteen minute or so drive up to the Alturas to get a good night's sleep. The Alturas was his primary place of refuge now and he often spent several days there to clear his head and try to figure out what was going wrong with his business and his marriage. He saw no reason to tell his wife where he went or what he was doing. This was not the behavior of a good husband, but in Jeske's mind, the marriage was already over. He was just too proud to admit defeat and take the next step.

By the second week of March, Elaine Jeske decided to take the next step herself and paid a visit to the law offices of Claude I. Parker and Ralph W. Smith. They drew up the necessary papers, including a property settlement that would allow Elaine to divorce her husband, John Jeske. The papers were signed and filed on March 25, 1935, with the agreement to meet in court on March 27th.[3] The day of the court appearance, Jeske signed a document that waived his right to appeal the divorce and to enter a default on his behalf. He wanted no part of the spectacle Elaine was setting up for him. In front of Superior Court Judge Leon R. Yankwich, Elaine, in her typically melodramatic fashion, sketched out the pain and anguish she felt from what she believed was Jeske's inability to function as a husband and play the part she wanted him to perform. Her mother, Gertrude, was there in the courtroom to provide her support. Elaine claimed her husband's behavior during their marriage was an example of "cruelty" and claimed Jeske "harassed and badgered" her for no apparent reason. "We are just not suited to each other," Elaine confessed. Jeske's side of the story was never told, and it appears he did not really care at that point. Elaine could say whatever she wanted as long as she stayed as far away from him as possible. The settlement was financially painful for an already "cash poor" Jeske. He lost what little savings he had as well as most of his personal possessions. The court granted the divorce on April 19, 1935, and it would become final a year from that date. There was nothing left for Jeske to do but pack his meager belongings and deposit them in his room at the Alturas for now.

It was a blessing when the summer months finally came around. The news in town was always bad, it seemed. In May, the Parkers were granted a re-trial on a technicality. The trial would take place in November and Jeske and his ex-wife would be required to appear. When June finally came, Jeske needed a release and he threw a few things in his Ford coupe and took off for the Sierra Nevada Mountains and his beloved cabin in Big Pine. Life was simple and uncomplicated there. There were no reminders of his unhappy life in Los Angeles to haunt him when he was in the mountains. The hardy folks who lived year round in Big Pine generally kept to themselves and made it a point not to bother the people who came to hunt or fish in their beautiful country. Jeske could go about his business without being harassed wherever he went. It was his idea of paradise. Unfortunately, fresh from the pain of his divorce and failing business venture, Jeske was having a hard time blending in and relaxing. He didn't feel like talking about his troubles, and yet he was lonely for some kind of companionship. Bob Logan had passed away and his widow sold the Glacier Pack Train Station to a couple named Wallace and Hazel Partridge earlier that year (1935).[4] The Partridges' 22-year-old son Kenneth helped his parent's take care of the place and run the business during the summer months. Jeske would frequently come to the station toward the evening hours to just talk and enjoy the company of some human beings. The Partridge family knew of Jeske from newspaper accounts of the deaths of Lon and Hazel Chaney and the subsequent kidnapping ordeal. They chose to keep the information to themselves for the most part, hoping that Jeske would one day open up to them and tell a little about his time with the famous actor and his wife.

It was clear from the beginning that Jeske had very little money and couldn't even afford to rent a horse to ride along the trails like he used to love doing back in the old days. A deal was struck that would provide a horse for Jeske to ride whenever he liked in exchange for doing some odd jobs around the stables. He wasn't quite rugged enough to be a packer, but Jeske helped to deliver horses to the packers who worked along the mountain trails. Young Kenneth worked closely with Jeske and eventually gained his trust. The young man talked with Jeske about many things during the warm summer days, and sometimes Jeske would even talk a little about his special friend, Lon Chaney. He always called him simply "Lon" and spoke with such a reverential respect that Kenneth could tell how much the older man had loved his friend. "Lon was a very nice man," Jeske would say with deep emotion. Jeske showed the young man a beautiful, heavily embossed leather saddle that had been a gift from Chaney to his "faithful friend." Kenneth knew from experience a custom saddle like that was a very expensive item. Jeske used it whenever he went for a ride along the trails above Glacier Lodge. He was always heavily armed and would say he was going "hunting," though he would inevitably return without a single kill. Even here in this glorious place Jeske could not escape the fear that he was being followed by members of Britton's gang and they would try to hurt him again. He wouldn't let it happen this time—he'd be ready for them.

Jeske spent the entire summer at his cabin purposely avoiding his responsibilities in Los Angeles and just about everything else. He remained alone there in the mountains. No parties with various Los Angeles guests like he used to have now and then during the time Chaney was alive. He had lost his taste for the Hollywood party scene after his experience with Elaine. All Jeske wanted now was some peace and quiet to think. He had all the time in the world to think.

By August he was forced to return to Los Angeles and the Alturas and face whatever music was playing for him there. It was clear that he was not a restaurateur or, frankly, a businessman of any kind. He just wanted to be left alone. Jeske talked it over with his elderly friend, Edward Henderson, and on August 20th it was decided that Henderson would buy back the Alturas business and try to run it again himself. Since Jeske still owed a considerable amount, the deal was mainly a wash just to get out from under the financial burden. It was also agreed that Jeske would be allowed to live there and help out as best he could in exchange for reduced room and board. There was a small rent to pay, but Henderson for once did not feel like taking advantage of the unfortunate man. Jeske's life was now reduced to hiding out in the mountains of Brentwood Heights during the winter, and in the mountains of Big Pine during the summer. He felt too paralyzed to even try to make a life for himself in town. Too many people knew him there—knew of his past with the Chaneys and the divorce. To make matters even worse, Lynden and Joy Parker received a special Christmas present when all charges were dropped against them and they were released from the County jail on December 24th. Would they come after him, or put some other group of thugs up to harassing him again? Jeske was nearing a nervous breakdown and unable to handle his everyday life. He couldn't even face going out and trying to get a job. Besides, what could he possibly do for a living? The skills he had learned from the master of make-up himself, Lon Chaney, were of no use to him now. If he went to the movie studio and begged for a job in the make-up department, it would be a betrayal of Chaney's trust. He had promised his friend to keep his involvement with the make-up work a secret to the grave, and Jeske intended to make good on his word. Unfortunately, that meant forever closing the door on the one chance he had for a real career. The decision was made when Chaney died, though, and he was not the kind of man who stabbed his friends in the back. Besides, he didn't want to have to face Creighton Chaney and relive all that angst. Some things were better left dead and buried.

The remainder of 1935 and much of the first part of 1936 was spent by Jeske in a sort of altered state of reality where he lived, yet did not really live at all. He was in a holding pattern waiting for something else to happen, someone else to try to take what was given to him by the Chaney's. It was a sad, dark place to be, but it was all Jeske had for now.

Across town, Elaine was living with her mother in a home they had built in North Hollywood up on Ridgemoor Drive in the summer of 1936. Thanks to her ex-husband's generous support, Elaine had the funds to buy the land and hire the contractor. It was a cute little bungalow with two bedrooms and a full bath—just enough room for Elaine and Gertrude. For a time, Elaine again used the name "Wilmont" to try to re-kindle some interest in her screenwriting career and deflect any undo scrutiny over her the sensational kidnapping experience and the recent messy divorce, which by now had been finalized. She was a free woman again, and had her eye on one of the handsome painters who worked on her new home. He was a Canadian transplant by the name of William Frederick Montgomery, who was easily manipulated by Elaine's persuasive feminine charms. It was hard being a woman alone and Elaine needed another playmate.

Creighton Chaney was having troubles of his own in 1936. His already-shaky marriage was beyond repair. Dorothy Chaney could no longer stand her husband's heavy drinking and abusive behavior. Dorothy testified in court on July 24, 1935 that Creighton's drinking was out of control and he frequently stayed out at night and refused to tell her where he'd been—testimony that was corroborated by Dorothy's father, Ralph L. Hinckley. The following day, the court not only granted her the divorce and custody of their two sons, Lon Ralph and Ronald Creighton, but awarded Dorothy nearly all of Creighton's worldly possessions in addition to 20% of everything he was to earn over $3,600 per year, with a cap of $1,200.[5] Creighton was virtually wiped out by the divorce and sought solace in the arms of his longtime girlfriend, Patsy Beck. Patsy tried to comfort Creighton as best as she could, even when he was drunk and violent. She understood his moods and was willing to do whatever it took to stay with him. In between the bouts of drunken rage he was a very kind person with a good heart and fun to be with. Creighton too often let his demons get the best of him and his depression became intolerable. He had to drink to stay sane, but this kind of sanity was only an illusion and a way to avoid dealing with the darker side of his nature. Patsy's calming influence helped to pull him out of this deep hole and the two would be married on October 1, 1937, in Colton, California. Creighton was so broke he could only afford a $6 silver band for a wedding ring. Desperate for work, Creighton finally broke down and did the one thing he had resisted for so long: He signed a new contract with Fox as "Lon Chaney, Jr." At least, he thought he would be able to get some new film jobs and make a living. For a time he would work hard to build a life for his new bride and revive his failing career, but even the love of a good woman couldn't save Creighton from himself.

By December of 1936, Jeske had exhausted what was left of his money reserves and he was forced to plead with his friend Ralph W. Smith to have Hazel's executor, Claude Parker, release some money from his inheritance so he could survive. The attorneys managed to cut a check to Jeske for $500 on December 10th to help keep him afloat for a while. Smith was one of the few friends Jeske had in the "real" world, and they would get together now and then to talk and enjoy a drink. Smith was a student of Eastern European cultures and languages, and had a few years earlier made and extensive tour of Russia returning home to give lectures at the Foreign Trade Club about Russia's business climate and opportunities.[6] With Jeske's background, Smith undoubtedly found a wealth of inside information regarding Russia and its territories.

Unbeknownst to Jeske, across the country in Detroit, Michigan, another tragedy had struck the Jeske family. John's older brother Carl—who had been going by the name "Charles" at this time—was attempting to make repairs one snowy night to a second-floor balcony at the home he shared with a German widow, Mathilde

Gerling. There was a considerable amount of ice and slush on the balcony, and Carl lost his footing and was pitched over the railing headfirst onto the pavement below. In a manner that was eerily reminiscent of his brother Julius' death in 1931, Carl died on December 10th of a massive skull fracture at the age of forty-seven. Mrs. Gerling made sure he was given a proper Christian burial in a plot she purchased for him in Detroit. He never spoke to her about his family, so she had no way to contact them. Carl never married and had no offspring, so his story abruptly came to an end there on that cold winter night.[7]

By the spring of 1937, Jeske would again be at the door of his attorney's office asking for another advance. This time he only received $250, but it would have to be enough. The alimony payments were proving difficult to make in addition to Jeske's other living expenses. By the summer, Jeske was relieved to once again get away from all the pressure and bask in the beauty of the tall pine trees and cool, inviting streams of Big Pine.

To Kenneth Partridge, Jeske was a well-built, rather rugged man tanned by hours spent in the sun. Someone he considered to be "a nice fellow . . . pretty tender-hearted; never angry at an animal or anything." When they talked, the younger man would often study his mysterious friend's features as he moved, and concluded there was indeed a striking resemblance to Lon Chaney—even the same size and build. He could understand how Jeske was able to double for Chaney in the movies and be his stand-in. This was the only revelation of his former life Jeske allowed past his lips during the five years he knew Kenneth and his family. Jeske never spoke of his ex-wife or any of the details of their life together. A little was said about the kidnapping and Jeske's continued fears of being stalked by some unnamed and unknown "gang" of thugs. The fear was very real to Jeske and he rarely traveled without a gun or a heavy flashlight to protect himself.

Jeske's one joy was to saddle his horse and ride the dirt trail up the mountain to where Chaney's stone cabin stood to fish in their favorite spot. The cabin's new owner, Ruluff Slimmer, was often there during the summer months and would greet Jeske warmly and chat about fishing and other things while having a smoke on the porch. In the evenings, Jeske would stay in his cabin and listen to the radio or some music on his portable record player. It was generally a very solitary, and very lonely, existence.

When Jeske arrived back in Los Angeles in September, he was forced to once again tap into his inheritance for money to keep him going a while longer. He didn't want to have to go through the ordeal of finding a "real" job, especially during the Depression. There were very few jobs to go around and a lot of unemployed, able-bodied men looking for work. Jeske was a divorced, forty-seven year-old man living out of a hotel room who hadn't been steadily employed in over three years. He didn't paint a very promising picture to a prospective employer at first glance. There would be another check for $500 on September 10th, and then another in November. Jeske's expenses must have been extremely high, considering the average three-bedroom house rented for under $50. Were the alimony payments taking up all his extra funds, or were there other business ventures as yet undisclosed? Jeske left no record of his activities during this time period other than the requests for funds he made to the attorney's office. There is evidence he was still sending money back east to his help his brother Gus out, considering the dire circumstances the elder Jeske found himself in. It's probably safe to say to assume that John never told Gus the full details of his troubles to somehow keep up the façade of affluence his brother believed he was continuing to enjoy. John couldn't bring himself to tell the whole sordid truth at a time when his brother needed something positive to hold on to. The 58-year-old bachelor lived in a small room he rented from a family of funeral directors, and was sick from the years of abuse his lungs had taken from working in the family bakery and the coal mines of Scranton, Pennsylvania. He rarely saw Julius' family, even though they only lived a few blocks from him. Gus wanted to be left alone and his family respected his wishes.

Elaine had worked her magic and convinced her new beau, Fred Montgomery, to get married. It would be the second marriage for the Canadian house painter and Elaine's third. Hopefully, she thought, the third time would be the charm. Elaine shaved a few years off her age to make herself seem a little more appealing to her 40-year-old husband, but time and the bottle had not been kind to her. The marriage took place in Los Angeles on October 9, 1937, and the newlyweds set up house at Montgomery's home in Burbank and hoped for the best. At least Jeske would be off the hook for the alimony now, but his future was also on very shaky ground.

As the news of Elaine's marriage reached Jeske, he was once again in financial difficulties. Jeske probably had the same attitude about his brief marriage to Elaine as her first husband, Paul Beuter—it was a "stupid marriage." What had he been thinking? Jeske was in serious turmoil and grief over the deaths of Lon and Hazel Chaney, and staring the prospects of a very lonely life in the face when he proposed to her. At first all seemed to be going so wonderfully well, but the realities of living with an emotionally unstable, alcoholic quickly snapped him out of his reverie.

February of 1938 would be the last time he would be able to tap into his "residuary legacy" from Hazel's estate. The check was $250 this time. Jeske had mentioned investing in bonds around the time he was kidnapped in 1934, so there is a possibility he was putting his money away in investments for himself, or possibly his brother Gus. His very tangible fear of being a victim again of the same gang of thugs who kidnapped and harassed him was still with Jeske in 1938 and would be forever a part of his everyday life. He made sure to keep a very low profile and stay well under the radar at all times. Jeske used to take pride in his right to vote, but he stopped exercising this right in order to keep himself off the registration list. His name was no longer in the telephone book—he probably didn't even have a phone these days. Jeske spent his time at the Alturas Hotel walking the trails alone or riding one of the horses through the dense forest. He had artistic ability, so one can imagine him working on some sketches or painting, or possibly taking photos. Jeske had learned to love photography from his dear friend Lon Chaney. At this time, Jeske had no friends to speak of, except for attorney Smith and old Mr. Henderson from the Alturas. There was no one he felt he could trust anymore. The days and nights all blended together and faded away into the horizon. Time seemed to be Jeske's enemy now.

The Thanksgiving of 1938 turned out to be a tragic time for many in the hills above Los Angeles. Five massive blazes swept through the hills and valleys of Topanga, San Antonio, Henderson, Day, and Waterman Canyon areas. High winds and very low humidity allowed the fires to burn uncontrolled for days, scorching scores of homes, outbuildings, and acres of brush land. A great many celebrities were forced to vacate their expensive homes, but thankfully, few were lost in the inferno. The biggest dollar loss was the exclusive Arrowhead Springs Hotel which was totally consumed in the blaze along with twenty-five neighboring homes. Two hundred extras on location in Topanga Canyon for a Hal Roach Studios film were getting ready to evacuate when they were all ordered to stay put by the Sheriff's office in case their services were needed in the fire fighting effort.[8] Chaney attorney and friend, Claude I. Parker, lost a storage shed and its contents, but his rambling horse ranch was untouched. By this time, Parker enjoyed breeding and training race horses more than the rat race of his former legal profession. It took nearly a week to contain the fires and much longer to clean up and try to repair the damage done. Dust clouds billowed over the affected areas as the wind whipped up the dirt left behind after the fire burned away the plants covering the hills and valleys.

As 1939 began, both Jeske and Creighton Chaney found themselves in financial turmoil. Creighton, or rather, "Lon, Jr.," was again without a studio contract and was nearly broke. The tide was about to turn for Lon's boy and he would soon embark on one of the most memorable film roles of his career: The simple-minded "Lennie" of John Steinbeck's novel *Of Mice and Men*. Creighton would first play the role on the stage at the El Capitan Theater in Los Angeles (as a replacement for Broderick Crawford. The two actors would later become close friends), and then on the screen in the United Artists film adaptation. *Of Mice and Men* was the big break Creighton was looking for and he had high hopes for the future. The same could not be said of Jeske. He continued to live in constant fear and had very little to hope for anymore.

A sense of fear and anxiety had also gripped the world as Adolph Hitler and his Nazi troops rolled into Poland in September of 1939. Poland had only enjoyed its autonomy as an independent nation for less than twenty-years before the horror or war and occupation reared its head once more. Hundreds of thousands of Poles would die in the ensuing chaos instigated by a madman with dreams of ethnically purifying the region and cleansing the entire world. Poland's former occupier, Russia, conspired with Germany at first, and the two nations signed a treaty dividing Poland into two parts. The Polish defenses were no match for the huge Nazi war machine, and the country soon fell to the Germans. Poland officially surrendered on September 29, 1939, plunging Eastern Europe into further bloodshed and terror. Little did Stalin know that Hitler would soon break the treaty and send his troops into Russia to cause widespread death and destruction. The United States at first declared its neutrality, but would later agree to send supplies to its allies Britain and France who were in a desperate fight to ward off the advancing Nazi forces. The entire world nervously watched and waited and felt sickened at the thought of another terrible war engulfing the globe once again.

Jeske must have also felt anguish and horror at the thought of the Nazi's methodical push to exterminate the Polish people along with all the other ethnic groups in the region—the Jews and Gypsies being the most persecuted. What had become of his parents and the sisters who stayed behind in Europe? Jeske would never know their fate, but could only imagine the turmoil that must have befallen his ethnically mixed family. Even with the heaviness in his heart, Jeske would again make the drive to Big Pine when the weather turned warmer, but money continued to be tight. Actually, there was a way to become solvent, and it was something that would break Jeske's heart and send his life even further into a tail spin of hopelessness.

In early 1940, Jeske sold his beloved mountain cabin in Big Pine— the cabin Lon Chaney had built for him— to an older couple named Robert and Emma Blake.[9] The Blakes were longtime residents of Big Pine and had wanted a cabin near Glacier Lodge for family members to enjoy. The Partridge family was getting ready to sell the Glacier Pack Train Station and move out of Big Pine. President Roosevelt enacted a full draft of young men on October 29, 1940. Kenneth had received his notice and was preparing to be shipped off to boot camp. Radical change was everywhere and Jeske's world continued to shrink and was in danger of collapsing around him. He would have to take drastic measures in order to survive—measures that would mean getting out in the world and trying to function normally again. Jeske had been out of the loop for so long he wasn't sure what to do. It was a lucky thing for him that he still had friends who could be of help to him in these dark days.

One such friend was Louis Mansey, the auto mechanic pal of Lon Chaney's who was responsible for bringing the actor and Jeske together way back when. Mansey was now a successful businessman with investments in Hollywood real estate. The Alturas was not a functioning business as of November of 1941 when the Kenter Canyon area was rezoned for single-family residences only. Henderson continued to live in the ranch home that had been the hotel and found ways to make a living without much concern for whether or not his methods were legal. Mansey and his wife Ona were able to offer Jeske a home at 1016 Laurel Avenue in West Hollywood. It was a comfortable, attractive two-bedroom bungalow in what was then a quiet residential neighborhood. Jeske moved in what few belongings he had left and set up house. The rent would be minimal in exchange for the upkeep of the home and the surrounding yard. For now, Jeske had a stable home base to make his attempt to rebuild his fractured life.

A new potential setback would shortly emerge when Jeske was informed that one of his kidnappers, Ida Mae Alameda, had been paroled from Tehachapi State Prison on November 17th and was living in the Los Angeles area. Ida Mae was given a job as a housekeeper and governess for a private family and struggled to make a new life for herself—free from the crime and domination she felt under Floyd Britton. A couple of years later, Ida Mae would write of her experiences: "It was so hazy and unreal. I was in a mental daze then . . . Britton did have some kind of hold on me—an infatuated youngster is what I was, and I can't give the slightest reason why. He threatened suicide if I left him—vowed he would marry [me] . . . All my family was disgusted with me because I was not married to him. In my mental state, all I was aware of was the possibility of getting married to him and then the rest would straighten out." Sadly, for Ida Mae, things did not "straighten out," but a seven-year stretch in prison did manage to put things in perspective for the still-young woman. She wanted no part of her former life of crime and never thought of the Jeske's or any of her past companions again.

On December 7, 1941, the "day that will live in infamy," Japanese fighters attacked U.S. forces on Pearl Harbor, emphatically ending the debate some Americans had of whether or not the U.S. should be involved in what seemed like another European war. President Roosevelt acted swiftly to declare war on Japan the following day, December 8th. With the declaration of war against the U.S. by Germany, the U.S. countered by declaring war on Germany on December 11th. Declarations of war were also issued against Hungary, Romania, and Bulgaria on December 12th. There was no turning back now, and the U.S. would be plunged headlong into another world war. Patriotic U.S. citizens worked together to keep the home front safe and to provide all the necessary materials and resources to help our fighting men as they shipped out overseas. It was a proud time to be a U.S. citizen, but a difficult and uncertain time for those of foreign birth and those who did not enjoy full citizenship. Back in June of 1940, FDR had signed into law the Smith Act which required all aliens to register and be fingerprinted. After the Japanese attack on Pearl Harbor, Japanese aliens and Japanese-Americans were eyed with suspicion and fear. Something would need to be done to secure the safety of the West Coast from further Japanese aggression.

There is something rather tragic and ironic about the fact that after so many years of unemployment, Jeske was finally able to secure a position with Bardwell & McAllister, at their facility on Santa Monica Boulevard. Up until the U.S. entered World War II, Bardwell & McAllister manufactured specialized lighting equipment for the motion picture industry. It is possible that an old friend of Lon Chaney's remembered Jeske and gave him a job as a belated favor. Thanks to FDR's "New Deal" and the creation of the Social Security system, Jeske was required to obtain a Social Security number now that he was on the payroll with B & A. He went down to the local government office and filled out the necessary application on December 12, 1941. It must have been a good feeling to have a job and be amongst the living again. Jeske's flush of success was short lived, as Bardwell & McAllister made the decision in 1942 to turn all of their plants over to the war effort and signed a government contract to produce parts for airplanes and other equipment. Some of their locations were temporarily shut down—Jeske's place of employment was one of them. With FDR's Executive Order, known as the "Japanese Internment Order," Japanese-Americans and Japanese aliens were rounded up and sent to what amounted to concentration camps away from the sensitive coastal areas that had been vulnerable to Japanese attack. Also targeted, though not as openly, were people of German and Italian decent, and many German-Americans were arrested and detained for questioning regarding their activities often based on hearsay and false information. Jeske's German background made him an easy target and unable to continue his work with Bardwell & McAllister after their changeover to government contracts. Jeske was let go of his position and forced back to square one again in his search for stability.

To make matters worse, Jeske lost the property in Placerville he had received in Hazel Chaney's will. He was so broke he could not afford to pay the property taxes, and the land was turned over to the State of California in June of 1942. Jeske had sold his property in Los Angeles and received some much-needed cash back in 1938, so it is unknown why he did not proceed with the sale of the lots in Placerville at the same time. Possibly, he had plans for the property—it was a beautiful location and a place where he could go to "hide out" if he needed to. Creighton Chaney had wanted this property and always resented the fact that Hazel gave it to Jeske. He had managed to keep tabs on it through his lawyer friend, Barry Woodmansee, with the hope that one day it would be in Chaney hands again. The forfeiture of the property by Jeske's inability to pay the property taxes was the open door Creighton had been waiting for, but it would take a number of years more before he would be able to make his move. Whatever Jeske's reasons were for not selling the land when he had the chance; he managed to hang on for six years before losing the property and any money he may have received from its sale. Jeske may have been so sick of the whole legal rigmarole, or possibly simply too mentally and physically exhausted to deal with any more issues relating to what must have seemed at this point as a "cursed" inheritance.

Elaine's try for a better life was turning to ashes before her eyes. In the letter she wrote to her then father-in-law in 1928 about her failing marriage, she stated that she was "selfish enough to want a catch at happiness." The happiness she sought always seemed to be just out of her reach, and her only solace continued to be the bottle. Her new marriage to house painter Fred Montgomery seemed off to a good enough start, even though the "deadly routine" of domesticity was ever present. At noon on March 23, 1942, it was time for lunch, and Fred began to make his way down the ladder he was working from. His foot slipped off the rung and he lost his grip just long enough to tumble off the ladder and hit the pavement below. Montgomery fell a long distance and hit the ground hard enough to crush his pelvis and fracture many other bones. He was rushed to the nearby hospital, but the prognosis wasn't good. Montgomery never regained consciousness and died the following day at the age of forty-three. Elaine was now a thrice-married widow with no prospects and nowhere to go but back to the home of her mother, Gertrude. Within a couple years, Elaine would grow weary of her beloved Hollywood and try to revitalize what was left of her life by packing up her belongings and moving to New Orleans.

Shortly before Christmas of 1942, the newspapers carried a story of a handful of convicts who were to have their sentences commuted by the outgoing governor, Culbert L. Olsen. One of these lucky gentlemen was former Jeske kidnapper, Cyril "Heavy" Russell, who had his sentence reduced to sixteen years. He was automatically eligible for parole and released from San Quentin Prison on January 28, 1943. Russell moved to the Sacramento area to pursue a job with a company that repaired and tested airplane radio equipment, and did not attempt to go back to Los Angeles.

Not long after Russell's parole, the main man behind the Jeske kidnapping plan, Floyd Britton, was finally paroled from San Quentin Prison on February 1, 1943. Britton had been the most vocal of his gang in trying to win his freedom, having put in many clemency requests over the years. In a letter written on May 24, 1937 to be included with his application for clemency, Britton insisted that he never understood why he was treated so severely when he didn't think his crime was all that bad—certainly not bad enough to warrant "special circumstances" and life in prison. The Jeskes may have been bound, gagged, and stuffed into an automobile for hundreds of miles and kept prisoner in a garage, but they weren't roughed up or anything: "Because of a finely drawn point, a crime that a few months prior would have been first-degree robbery became "kidnapping with torture." The Superior Court definitively decided that physical torture was not indicated in any respect. The torture was plainly stated as 'mental agony.' Mental agony: I know about that. . . ." Britton went on to share a little insight into his former life of crime: "Something within me died. I had no heart for anything—to the casual observer I appeared as just another young man, but inside of my head only chaos was evident. Blinded to every moral obligation, I let passion and emotion overwhelm me. I made friends among people I had little business with; a good fellow or a witty woman seemed to dull the perpetual ache. Perhaps the universal disgust I had for normal existence was but a suppressed disgust with my own self. At any rate, I thought I simply did not care." Britton would also make a home for himself in Sacramento and attempted to reconcile with his wife and young son. He would manage to stay out of trouble and had no desire to venture back to his old haunts in the Los Angeles Area, or look up his former flame, Ida Mae Alameda. She wouldn't have wanted him back anyway. Ida Mae had a new life now and a new home in Fresno and had met a young service man named Eugene V. Hardy. They were married on September 16, 1943, and enjoyed eighteen months of marriage before Hardy was shipped out for duty overseas. His tour of duty was cut short a year later when he was diagnosed with a congenital heart defect and honorably discharged. Ida Mae would have to go back to working as a waitress to make ends meet. Hardy was never physically very strong and would die in 1955.

With three main members of the gang of thugs who had so horribly abused him and subjected him and his then-wife Elaine to all sorts of indignities and mental anguish out of prison and free to possibly attack him again, Jeske's paranoia reached a new high in 1943 and the stress on his physical well-being was beginning to take its toll. He had trouble sleeping, was losing weight, and spent a good deal of time locked behind the door of his bungalow on Laurel Avenue. His attorney friend, Ralph W. Smith, did his best to keep Jeske's spirits up, and may have been behind the offer of employment for Jeske to work for the County of Los Angeles. It wasn't a glamorous job by any means, but Jeske wasn't in the position to refuse the work. Jeske would use his driving skills to move a truck of road repairing materials to wherever the road maintenance crew needed the supplies. The date he started working for the county isn't known, but even this position would not last long for Jeske. He was now fifty-three years-old and had nothing to show for his life—

his once-magical life with Lon and Hazel Chaney. All that was left to him now were his memories and his continuing sense of loyalty to the one true friend he ever had. Chaney's secrets would never be revealed during Jeske's lifetime—the "faithful servant" made sure of it.

Rationing of essential products—gasoline, coffee, shoes, meat, cheese, and other items—had begun in the U.S. in 1942 and continued on until the end of the war in 1945. In May of 1944, meat rationing ended, except for certain prime cuts of meat. The wily old businessman, Edward Henderson, had made good money out of providing illegal cuts of meat to the public through the Alturas up in Kenter Canyon. For some, the war brought excellent business opportunities and Henderson wasn't one to miss a good thing when it came his way.

May was also the time of another tragedy for the Jeske family. It was a beautiful, warm spring in California—the time of year usually reserved for new beginnings of all kinds. This year— 1944—it would be a new beginning of another kind for Jeske. He had been feeling more tired lately and more lethargic than usual, and his mind was continuously tormented by wild thoughts of nameless thugs who were just waiting to do him harm. On the evening of Wednesday, May 10th, Jeske was feeling agitated and he didn't want to be alone. Ralph W. Smith could hear the tension in his friend's voice over the phone and agreed to come over to see if he could calm him down. Smith drove over to Jeske's home on Laurel Avenue and sat down with his friend to talk over a cup of coffee and a good cigar. No record was left of the details of the conversation, no clue as to what it was that caused Jeske to be especially fearful and agitated this particular evening. By late in the evening—around 10 or 11 PM—Jeske seemed to be in mild distress, but nothing to be too alarmed about. Possibly it was something he ate that didn't agree with him. Suddenly, without warning, Jeske slumped over in his chair—dead. It was a quick and painless death—no struggling or even time for a last word. Jeske was gone, and so were all the many secrets his memory held of Lon Chaney. All the little things he could have told about Lon Chaney, the man, as well as Chaney, the great actor and make-up artist. Jeske knew it all, yet he kept the details deep inside his heart, never to be revealed.

Smith tried in vain to revive his friend, but could see it was useless. He picked up the phone and called the local Sheriff's office. By Midnight a Deputy from the Coroner's office was there along with a Sheriff's Deputy to take down the details of what had happened and move Jeske's body downtown. It was already the next day, May 11th, by the time the coroner's office removed Jeske's belongings—$28.20 in cash, a pair of horn rim glasses, a wallet with miscellaneous cards, and a St. Regis pocket watch— and placed him in the examining room. A doctor, J. L. Robinson, was on hand to review the case and make his determination as to the cause of death. The curious thing about this episode is that Dr. Robinson was able to ascertain Jeske's death was due to "chronic myocarditis" without doing an autopsy.[10] Had Jeske been taking medication for this viral heart ailment? Did Smith know of his friend's medical history and was able to tell the coroner's office? There was no coroner's report, so no further details are available to shed light on this mysterious situation. Later investigation revealed some members of the Jeske family suffered from a genetic heart defect that took the life of a handful of relatives over the years.[11] John Jeske could have had such a defect that was never detected and misdiagnosed at the time. The enormous amount of stress Jeske was under for the last fourteen years of his life must have significantly contributed to the damage done to his already-weak heart. Only three days before his death, Jeske celebrated his fifty-fourth birthday. His life had been cut short by tragedy and loss and disappointments. The story wasn't quite over yet, though, as even Jeske's death would be the scene for more ill fortune.

Ralph W. Smith stepped in to help his deceased friend and established himself as the executor of Jeske's "estate." Sadly, though, there was no real estate to manage, as Jeske died intestate and without any real assets. Here is where the mystery deepens: Smith knew of Jeske's inheritance—the property, the bonds, and the cash—yet it seemed to have disappeared by the time of Jeske's death. Jeske's body was embalmed and held by the Utter-McKinley Mortuary on Sunset Boulevard a full twenty-two days—but why? The quick answer would be that there was no money to bury Jeske and the mortuary was working to try to find a relative or someone who could put up the funds to give the poor man a proper burial. A memorial service was held at 3 p.m. on Friday, May 19th at the mortuary. Was Elaine there? Creighton Chaney, perhaps? It is doubtful that many attended this final farewell to a man few had ever known well.

Where was Smith during the time Jeske's body laid in storage at the mortuary? During the many conversations he had had with Jeske, it would be plausible to suggest Jeske had told him at least about his brother Gus back in Pennsylvania. There is evidence to suggest that Gus was known to Smith, but there is no evidence that anyone ever notified Gus or any other Jeske family member that John had died. On June 1st, Utter-McKinley finally struck a deal with the Inglewood Park Cemetery to take Jeske's body and lay him to rest. He was buried on that day in an unmarked grave— unmourned and forgotten. Jeske's legacy would be in his undeniable loyalty and trust in his one true friend, Lon Chaney, and Chaney's wife Hazel. Both treated him with the respect and kindness Jeske would never find again in his short life. Whether or not Jeske would want to be remembered is doubtful. If only Jeske had left more of himself behind, there would not be such rampant speculation as to his methods and motives, or the malicious attempts to make him out to be some kind of monster. He was neither angel nor devil—only a man with good heart and a lot of latent talent who was given a chance to be more than he ever thought possible by one of the greatest actors Hollywood ever produced—Lon Chaney.

May he finally rest in peace.

Epilogue[1]

There is a story that has been handed down in the Jeske family that relates an incident that supposedly occurred sometime in 1943 or 1944 (possibly around the time John Jeske died) involving Lon Chaney, Jr. and a member of Jeske's family. Details such as time and place are non-existent, unfortunately, but I believe it important to tell the story simply because of the remarkable fact it has stayed alive for so many years. While Lon, Jr. was traveling across country by train with other Hollywood celebrities on one of their war bond drives, he stopped in Scranton, Pennsylvania—a stronghold of the Jeske clan. John Jeske's niece Freda married Benjamin Hollenback on February 3, 1940. Hollenback had a problem with alcohol and gained a reputation for having a bad temper when under the influence. For reasons as yet unknown, but somehow linked to John Jeske, Ben Hollenback was there to meet Lon, Jr. when he got off the train in Scranton. As soon as Hollenback saw the actor get off the train, he rushed forward, exchanged a few heated words, then hauled off and punched Lon Jr. square in the face. The actor was understandably dazed and confused by this assault, but appears to have done nothing in his defense. Hollenback died in the 1950s and his widow Freda, though saddened at her loss, felt a certain sense of relief to see him go. By the time I was able to talk to her (2005), her memory was not reliable and she could not even remember being married to Hollenback—or possibly she just did not want to remember. Whether or not this incident ever really happened will forever remain a mystery.

Four years after his death—in February of 1948—John Jeske's name was once more in the courts. Creighton Chaney, now using the name "Lon Chaney, Jr." in both his private and professional life, finally seized the opportunity to obtain the five lots located in Placerville, California bequeathed to Jeske in Hazel Chaney's will he had for so long desired for himself. The lots included a beautiful ranch home and property he wanted to use as his getaway spot from the pressures of Hollywood living. With the help of his lawyer friend Barry Woodmansee, it was discovered the property taxes had not been paid, and all that was required was for someone to pay the back taxes and they would have ownership of the land. Lon, Jr. paid the taxes in the name of the "Lon Chaney Estate" on August 1st of 1947. In order to gain title to the land, Jeske would first need to be eliminated as the rightful owner, and the only way to do so would be through probating his estate. An associate of Woodmansee's— Marie Peters—was set-up as Administratix of Jeske's estate on February 13, 1948. No mention is made of what became of Ralph W. Smith (he would die of a heart attack while on vacation in Boston in August of 1950), or why he was no longer involved as the executor. Peters claims in her petition Jeske had no living relatives, nor did he have any assets to speak of when he died, except for the property. Gustav "Gus" Jeske had passed away on November 20, 1947, at the age of sixty-nine. He had spent the last thirty days or so of his life in a hospital that treated mainly the indigent suffering from the lung disease that had made living a difficult and tiring proposition. Gus had been cared for by a kind nurse, Alice O'Boyle, who made sure he was properly buried in the nearby Shady Lane Cemetery. The family of funeral directors Gus had lived with took care of the arrangements and paid off his creditors. None of his family was at the hospital or the graveside to say "goodbye," nor did they even know when he had died until decades later.

Even with Gus dead and buried, it would appear Peters' search in February of 1948 was only half-hearted, since there were still a few people—Smith being one of them—who had known Jeske well enough to provide some personal information. Meanwhile, Lon, Jr., through his lawyer Woodmansee, filed an action in El Dorado County on April 10th to obtain a "quiet title" to the Placerville property. Peters is summoned to appear on April 19th, but fails to show up in court (as was part of the plan), which is entered as a default. In a morbid twist to the story, Lon, Jr., who had been suffering from debilitating depression for years, attempted to take his own life on April 22nd. He sat in his pickup truck and took a large amount of pills, washing them down with alcohol. His young son, Ronald, found him and ran back to the house to have his mother call for an ambulance. The unconscious actor was rushed to the hospital where doctors were able to save his life.[2] The Chaney family has so far declined to say what caused Lon Jr. to make this suicide attempt at this seemingly productive period in his life. Their privacy should be respected.

Two years later, on February 20, 1952, Peters files the necessary papers to be dismissed as administratrix of Jeske's estate saying her duties had been fulfilled. She went on to report Jeske had sold his rights to the land in Placerville to the State "years ago" (no definite date was given). This smoothed the way for Lon, Jr.'s suit in El Dorado County, and he was awarded title to the property on September 22, 1952. Two of the lots were immediately given to Woodmansee and his brother Patrick.

Former kidnapper George Dorsey (aka Jerry Lamaroux) had proven himself unworthy for parole in the 1940s (it had been granted and then revoked), but was finally released from Folsom prison on parole in 1951. No further information was available as to his fate.

Jeske's ex-wife Elaine saw her life continue to disintegrate into more booze-soaked unhappiness. She married again in Glendale, just outside of Los Angeles, to an Italian-American barber originally from New York named Frank Louis D'Aquino on January 22, 1946. Once again, Elaine lied about her age and this time lied about the number of times she had been married. Her place of birth also inexplicably changed from Wisconsin to Illinois. D'Aquino had left his ex-wife and young son, Vincent, behind in New York when he headed out west to try his luck in the balmy climate of Southern California. His luck obviously turned sour when he ran into Elaine, and their marriage did not last more than a few years. By 1949, Elaine was single again and writing a pitiful letter from her temporary home in Florida to former husband Paul Beuter asking if it would be possible to get together again. She wrote that she had always loved him and had "never cared for anyone like you." Beuter was remarried and doing well in San Francisco. He wanted nothing to do with this pathetic woman who had caused so much mental anguish. Elaine eventually found another man to marry—someone named Johnson—and moved back to Los Angeles in the late 1950s. In July of 1959, her obsession with Beuter led her to once again write (Mr. Johnson appears to have passed away at some point— probably necessitating her move back to California). She hoped he would visit her and her ailing mother sometime when he was down their way. The reunion would never take place. Grace Elaine Johnson (neé Cadwallader) died on May 23, 1965 of acute chronic alcoholism at the Los Angeles General Hospital. Her mother, Gertrude, passed away in 1961, and Elaine had been totally on her own for the first time in her life.

1961 was also a bad year for the Alturas Hotel. The hotel had long ago been occupied as a private, family residence. On November 6, 1961, the Santa Monica Mountains above Los Angeles would once again be the site of a horrible inferno that devastated the well-heeled communities of Bel Air and Kenter Canyon. Over 250 homes were lost, and the Alturas was among of the unlucky ones. It burned to the ground along with the other outbuildings that had once been the Alturas Country Club. As with all the things that had touched the life of John Jeske, there is nothing tangible left of the Alturas or its history.

Photo Gallery

Jeske brothers circa 1910: (L-R) Julius, Karl, Gustav, and Julius' wife/cousin, Christina (Courtesy of Robert Jeske)

Louis Mansey's auto repair shop on Santa Monica Blvd. circa 1923. Mansey is in the middle. (COURTESY OF LAURA ANDERSON)

Newspaper photo showing Lon Chaney embarking on a publicity tour for *The Hunchback of Notre Dame* in 1923. (L-R): Creighton, John, Lon, and Hazel Chaney, and an unidentified well-wisher.

On the set of *Phantom of the Opera*, circa 1925: (L-R) Isadore Bernstein, Norman Kerry and John Jeske, who is holding one of Chaney's prosthetic devices. (Courtesy of Philip J. Riley)

Grace Elaine and first husband Paul Beuter, circa 1927 (Courtesy of Lauren Peterlin)

Composite photo using a candid shots of Lon Chaney (circa 1927) and John Jeske (1934) to illustrate the strong resemblance between the two men.
(COURTESY OF THE AUTHOR)

Newspaper photo of Lon Chaney's casket being taken to his final resting place. Pallbearers include John Jeske, Clinton Lyle, and Ralph Hinckley.

1314 N. Hayworth Ave., Los Angeles: Home to Hazel Chaney and John Jeske from about 1931 until Hazel's death in 1933. (COURTESY OF THE AUTHOR)

Photo of Hazel Chaney taken after Lon's death in 1930. (COURTESY OF THE LOS ANGELES EXAMINER COLLECTION, DOHENY MEMORIAL LIBRARY, UNIVERSITY OF SOUTHERN CALIFORNIA)

4649 Beverly Blvd., Los Angeles: The Dover Apartments was home to John and Elaine Jeske throughout their brief marriage. Their one-bedroom apartment, #507, has been made into a studio, but there have been few changes since the Jeske's lived there. (COURTESY OF THE AUTHOR)

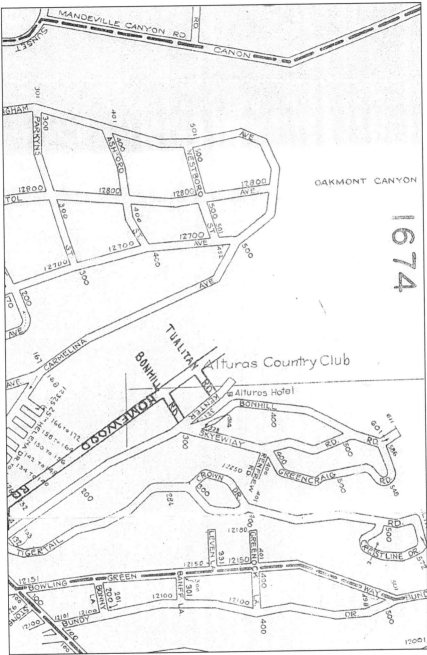

Detail of official Los Angeles County Precinct Map from January of 1936. The Alturas Country Club and Alturas Hotel are clearly marked as being off of Kenter Ave. The map contains a few errors—the country club was actually the area where the "Alturas Hotel" name is printed parallel to Bonhill Rd.

John Jeske's cabin in Big Pine, California as it looked in May of 2005.
(COURTESY OF DANIEL DOYLE)

John and Elaine Jeske standing in front of John's new, blue Ford V8 coupe in 1934. Handwritten note on back suggests photo was taken to be used in connection with a news story. (COURTESY OF ALICE BRINK)

Portrait photo taken of John Jeske by a *Los Angeles Examiner* reporter in July of 1934 in Jeske's Beverly Blvd. apartment. (COURTESY OF THE LOS ANGELES EXAMINER COLLECTION, DOHENY MEMORIAL LIBRARY, UNIVERSITY OF SOUTHERN CALIFORNIA)

Nearly full-length portrait taken during the same session in July of 1934. Notice the oil portrait of Elaine on the wall (most likely painted by Jeske). Jeske is leaning on the desk he received from Hazel Chaney in her will. (COURTESY OF THE LOS ANGELES EXAMINER COLLECTION, DOHENY MEMORIAL LIBRARY, UNIVERSITY OF SOUTHERN CALIFORNIA)

John and Elaine Jeske listening intently to testimony during the 1934 kidnapping trial. (COURTESY OF THE LOS ANGELES EXAMINER COLLECTION, DOHENY MEMORIAL LIBRARY, UNIVERSITY OF SOUTHERN CALIFORNIA)

Close-up of Joy Parker giving her testimony on the stand during the 1934 Jeske kidnapping trial. (COURTESY OF THE LOS ANGELES EXAMINER COLLECTION, DOHENY MEMORIAL LIBRARY, UNIVERSITY OF SOUTHERN CALIFORNIA)

Waiting for their turn to testify during the 1934 Jeske kidnapping trial: (L-R) George Dorsey, Lynden Parker, and Cyril Russell. (COURTESY OF THE LOS ANGELES EXAMINER COLLECTION, DOHENY MEMORIAL LIBRARY, UNIVERSITY OF SOUTHERN CALIFORNIA)

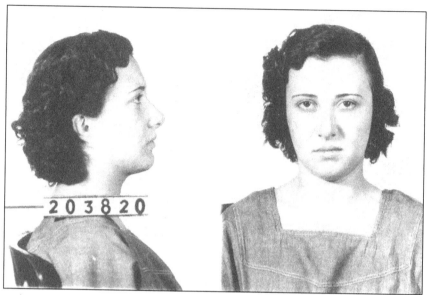

Mug shot of Ida Mae Alameda taken in 1934. (COURTESY OF THE CALIFORNIA STATE ARCHIVES)

Mug shot of Floyd Britton taken in 1934. (COURTESY OF THE CALIFORNIA STATE ARCHIVES)

Endnotes

CHAPTER 1: NEW BEGINNINGS AND GLIMPSES OF THE PAST:

1. Very little is known about the Jeske family's Eastern European origins. A search was made of the Russian State Historic Archive in St. Petersburg and the Grodzisk Mazowiecki archive in Poland for records of Friedrich Jeske and his family. No information could be found in either the civil or church records. Birthdates for only the brothers are known: Gustav, April 10, 1878; Julius, December 4, 1879, and Karl, March 15, 1889. All but one of the sisters (Adele) married, but no further information about their lives has surfaced.

2. The Geschichtswerkstatt Herrenwyk, or Historical Workshop, Herrenwyk, is a living museum just outside of Lübeck, Germany designed to give their visitors an idea of what it was like for the men who toiled at the metal fabricating plant and their families beginning in the year 1906. The museum's exhibits mainly cover the 1920s and 1930s, but information regarding all years is available.

3. Details of Friedrich's immigration contained in the ship's manifests, and specifics about the *S. S. Pennsylvania*, were gathered from the Ellis Island Project web site: www.ellisisland.org.

4. Scranton [PA] City Directory for 1912.

5. Michigan Department of Health—Certificate of Death, November 10, 1936. Name on the Certificate is "Carl Jaske," but there is a note saying "Also Jeske." Karl used the first name "Charles" occasionally (the 1911 Scranton City Directory lists him as "Charles Jeski," and was listed in the 1920 U.S. Federal Census report for Detroit as "Charles Jeshkie."

6. Interview with Laura Anderson, February 17, 2005. Mrs. Anderson is Louis Mansey's niece. Louis and Ona Mansey did not have any children, and Laura remained close to her Uncle and Aunt throughout their lives. Louis passed away in 1968, and Ona followed in 1976.

7. John (Jonathan) Chaney described his younger brother's behavior in his early days to journalist Adela Rogers St. Johns as being "nervous, high-strung, worried half to death all the time about money, with a pretty nasty temper." — *Liberty Magazine*, May 9, 1931, "Lon Chaney: A Portrait of the Man Behind a Thousand Faces."

8. Journalist Homer Currie wrote a fascinating piece for *Motion Picture* magazine's September 1925 issue called "The Uncanny Mr. Chaney." Chaney's abilities to analyze a person's character and the minute details of what he based his opinions on were discussed at length. Eliza Schallert noted that Chaney was "extremely instinctive and intuitive. If he likes you, you immediately know it. He may even tell you so. If he doesn't like you . . . you will have evidence of that too—promptly." (*Picture Play*, July 1927).

9. Chaney's ambition was revealed to Maude S. Cheatham and published in her article "Meet the Frog" for the March 1920 issue of *Motion Picture Classic* magazine. Adela Rogers St. Johns noted Chaney's early eagerness to talk to her about his make-up techniques when they first met on a movie set in 1916 (*Liberty Magazine*, May 16, 1931, "Lon Chaney: A Portrait of the Man Behind a Thousand Faces").

10. Hallet Abend, "An Interview in Verse with Lon Chaney," *Los Angeles Times*, February 25, 1923.

11. There seems to be some debate as to Lon Chaney's true adult height and weight. The 1923 *Blue Book of the Screen* directory describes Chaney as being 5'9 1/2" and 165 lbs. The following year, *Stars of the Photoplay* has him down to 5'9" and 155 lbs. By 1930, he had added an inch to stand 5'10", but was still a very svelte 155 lbs (*Stars of the Photoplay*). My personal belief is that he may have been 5'10" in heels, but in his stocking feet he was closer to about 5'7". John Jeske's height and description was listed in strikingly different ways on the two ship's manifests from 1912. The first one (March 26, 1912) had him as being 5'7", fair complexion, with black hair and brown eyes. The second one (April 7, 1912) listed a 5'9" man with a fair complexion, dark blonde hair and blue eyes (this description fits his brother Karl, oddly enough). The clerk who filled out Jeske's Declaration of Naturalization form at the Los Angeles courthouse on September 2, 1920 saw a man who was 5'9", 165 lbs., with a dark complexion, dark brown hair and brown eyes. Jackie Cooper, who worked with Chaney as a diminutive seven-year-old boy, remembered his co-star as being a "very short man." Adela Rogers St. Johns was the first journalist to note the resemblance between Chaney and Jeske in print in her 1931 *Liberty Magazine* biography of Chaney: "Jeske had the same build, the same deep lines in his face, the same quick black eyes." Actor Harry Earles—who played "Tweedledee" in both the 1925 and 1930 versions of *The Unholy Three* –told author Michael Blake in 1985 that Jeske "bore a strong resemblance to Chaney" (*Lon Chaney: The Man Behind the Mask*, pg. 199). Photographs do attest to this resemblance (see photo section).

12. Adela Rogers St. Johns describes how she watched Jeske help Chaney don his costume for *The Hunchback of Notre Dame* in her 1978 autobiography, *Love, Laughter and Tears: My Hollywood* Story (pg. 196). One curious comment comes from a 1961 interview with author Nathanial Ross where San

Francisco based make-up artist Leslie Carter claims to have helped Chaney design his costume for the hunchback. Carter also claims there were other artists involved in the process as well (*Lon Chaney: Master Craftsman of Make Believe*, 1981, self-published, page 123). No evidence has yet surfaced to back up this claim by Carter.

13. There were many published accounts of Chaney's dislike of any sort of pretension or the appearance of being "high-tone," such as the comment made by Lee Shippey in his interview with Chaney for his "The Lee Side o' L.A." column published in the *Los Angeles Times* on February 23, 1930, in which he states that Chaney is "scornful of the idea of having a valet and drives his own cars, of which he has only three." Chaney made these comments even though Jeske had been in his employ as a chauffeur and dresser (valet?) for the past seven years.

14. Adela Rogers St. Johns, *Love, Laughter and Tears: My Hollywood Story*, page 187. The interview with Cleva Creighton Bush was conducted in 1931 for her *Liberty Magazine* biography of Chaney. This quote was not used in the magazine article. Cleva was born Frances Cleveland Creighton in Kansas in August of 1888 to John Evans Creighton and Martha ("Mattie") Jane Johnson.

15. According to author Michael Blake, the marriage records for Oklahoma City, Oklahoma show that Lon and Cleva were married on May 31, 1906, and this fact was corroborated by a publication of the marriages for this date that appeared in the *Daily Oklahoman* newspaper on June 1, 1906. Creighton Tull Chaney was born on February 10, 1906 (*Lon Chaney: The Man Behind the Mask*, pgs. 21 – 22).

16. This letter was first published in an edited form on May 9, 1931 in Adela Rogers St. Johns biography of Lon Chaney for *Liberty Magazine*. The complete contents of the letter can be found in Nathanial Ross's 1981 self-published biography of

Chaney, *Lon Chaney: Master Craftsman of Make Believe*, on pages 54 – 55, and in Michael Blake's 1993 biography *Lon Chaney: The Man Behind the Mask*, pages 40 – 41.

17. Chaney alleged that Cleva had committed adultery on at least four occasions, and was able to provide names and dates (details can be found in *Lon Chaney: Master Craftsman of Make Believe*, by Nathanial Ross on pages 57 – 58, and *Lon Chaney: The Man Behind the Mask*, by Michael Blake, pages 39 – 40). Obviously, either Chaney was following Cleva unbeknownst to her, or he had paid someone to shadow her in order to obtain the evidence he needed to divorce her. The charges of adultery were dismissed, but the charge of "habitual intemperance" won Chaney his freedom and custody of his son.

18. The letter from Cleva to Lon was published in the *Los Angeles Times* under the title "Wife's Plea: Would See Her Child" on April 2, 1914. The later comments were made by Cleva to journalist Adela Rogers St. Johns in 1931, at a time when she says she felt no bitterness towards Lon. When she saw her words published in the May 9, 1931 issue of *Liberty Magazine*, her tone quickly changed. According to author Michael Blake, Cleva was furious over how she was portrayed in this article and wanted to sue, but didn't have a legal leg to stand on. She would go on to write her own version of what happened, *sans* any references to her infidelity, and claimed Lon had wanted her to have an abortion when he learned she was pregnant with Creighton (*A Thousand Faces: Lon Chaney's Unique Artistry in Motion Pictures*, page 20).

19. There are conflicting stories regarding whether or not Creighton saw his mother right after the divorce, and if it was really true that his father told him Cleva was dead. Cleva's comments to Adela Rogers St. Johns in 1931 make it sound like Lon would not let her see Creighton, even though the judge had given her visitation rights. In her 1969 autobiography, *The Honeycomb* (page 116), St. Johns quoted Cleva as saying

"I looked in the windows and [Lon] said he'd have me arrested" when she tried to catch a glimpse of her son Creighton. Author Nathanial Ross wrote that in 1973, Creighton Chaney told him he was "always permitted to see his mother in strict compliance with the court ruling" (**Lon Chaney: Master Craftsman of Make Believe**, page 59). It seems safe to say that Lon Chaney never saw his first wife again, and he allowed people (encouraged, even) to believe Creighton was his child by his second wife, Hazel.

20. Maud Robinson Toombs, "Lon Chaney: Collector of Faces," *Photo-Play Journal*, March 1921, page 20.

21. One of the first director's to work with Chaney, Allan Dwan, spoke of Chaney's early penchant for make-up, and how he quickly caught Dwan's attention (Nathanial Ross, *Lon Chaney: Master Craftsman of Make Believe*: Page 64 – 65).

22. Adela Rogers St. Johns: "Lon Chaney: A Portrait of the Man Behind a Thousand Faces" — *Liberty Magazine*, May 16, 1931, page 28. Hazel was born Marie Genevieve Hazel Bennett in San Francisco, California on April 25, 1887 to Charles H. Bennett and Louise M. Cella.

23. Lon, Hazel, and Creighton first lived at 1530 Hudson Avenue. At the beginning of the year 1920, the family was living on N. Edgemont Street where they shared their home with Hazel's brother Charles B. Bennett, his wife Maude, and an "uncle" named Roy Millard. Hazel's sister Eleanor Grace Lechert also had a son named "Roy Millard" by a first marriage, so the census record is puzzling.

24. Chaney had played a wide variety of roles prior to *The Miracle Man*, including a hunchbacked fisherman and a beast-like wild man, but "The Frog" was the first role that required more physical than cosmetic alterations to create the characterization.

25. The shoulder injury was reported by Dan Thomas in his syndicated—and hastily thrown together—obituary for Lon Chaney published in six installments in various newspapers nationwide beginning around August 28, 1930 under the title "The Life Story of Lon Chaney," and was repeated by others thereafter. There are many published accounts—both contemporary and post-mortem—of Chaney sustaining injury to his back, neck, legs, and other body parts for the sake of his art. Some are true, and others are the fabrication of wily publicity men and women. There are enough reports from Chaney's colleagues regarding his obvious discomfort and suffering while making certain pictures to believe that he did indeed go to Hell and back to achieve some of his most unusual characterizations in films like *The Miracle Man, The Penalty, The Hunchback of Notre Dame, The Phantom of the Opera, The Unknown,* to name but a few.

26. When asked about his experience making *The Penalty*, Chaney said, "We had to stop every few minutes to remove the straps and message my legs which had grown numb. The pain was pretty tough." — Dan Thomas, "The Life Story of Lon Chaney, Pt. 2," September 1930. A more graphic description of his alleged suffering can be found in Dorothy Donnell's article "A Martyr to the Movies?" from the December 1930 edition of *Motion Picture* magazine.

27. "'Blizzard' Most Difficult Role," *Douglas* [WY] *Enterprise*, May 31, 1921.

28. In 1927, a protégé of Chaney's, Cecil Holland, published a textbook on make-up called "The Art of Make-up for Stage and Screen" (Cinemax Publishing, Co.). Chaney wrote a lengthy foreword to the tome in which he noted Holland as being the one to create the first "office of staff make-up expert" at MGM Studios, which would be the forerunner of their full make-up department. Chaney ended his comments with a warning to fledgling artists: "Remember that this textbook is a tool—and how you use it depends on yourself.

Careful study of its facts, and careful application of them to original problems is your stepping stone to possible fame—or at any rate to the joy of knowing, in your own heart, that you are, as an actor, a competent workman."

29. Frank Chaney and Emma Kennedy were married on December 6, 1877 in Colorado Springs, Colorado, where they would raise four children: Jonathan Orange, August 5, 1879; Leonidas (Lon) Frank, April 1, 1883; Caroline Emma Alice, December 20, 1888; and George Leonidas, June 10, 1893. Another son, Earl, was born on May 14, 1887 but lived less than two months. Emma's parents, John and Mary Kennedy, founded the Colorado School for the Deaf in 1874. Frank Chaney worked for many years as a barber at the Antlers Hotel.

30. Adela Rogers St. Johns: "Lon Chaney: A Portrait of the Man Behind a Thousand Faces," *Liberty Magazine*, May 23, 1931. St. Johns referred to Jeske as Chaney's "dresser" for the first time in her 1978 autobiography, *Love, Laughter and Tears: My Hollywood Story*, (page 195) and describes the process Chaney went through to transform himself into "Quasimodo" with the help of Jeske (page 196). Author Robert G. Anderson described Jeske as Chaney's "chauffeur and valet" (*Faces, Forms, Films: The Artistry of Lon Chaney*, page 63).

31. Chaney and his wife had a very rich social life composed of a handful of close, trusted friends. In contrast to his personal life, Chaney tended to keep pretty much to himself while working. If he did socialize at all, it would have been with the stage hands or his beloved studio musicians Jack and Sam Feinberg.

Chapter 2: Lon Chaney's "Faithful Servant" and His Secrets

1. Telephone interview with Kenneth Partridge on June 15, 2005. As a teenager, Mr. Partridge worked at the Glacier Pack Train Station in Big Pine, California his parents owned from

about 1935 – 1941. He knew John Jeske at a time when Jeske was hiding out at his cabin during the summer months (see Chapter 5). Mr. Partridge said that Jeske told him he had been Chaney's stand-in.

2. James L. Howard, D.D.S., described how he developed the idea for Chaney's dentures in an article published in *Oral Hygiene* magazine (published after Chaney's death). See pages 122 – 123 of Michael Blake's Chaney biography, *A Thousand Faces.*

3. "Chaney as Himself Is Revelation": *Los Angeles Times*, August 10, 1924.

4. "Lon Chaney: A Portrait of the Man Behind a Thousand Faces": *Liberty Magazine*, May 23, 1931.

5. Ibid.

6. Universal manager William Sistrom said this to Chaney after the actor had gone to him in 1918 asking for a raise to $125 per week (*Photoplay*, February 1928: "The True Life Story of Lon Chaney").

7. *The Making of The Phantom of the Opera*, by Philip Riley: Page 40.

8. "Lee Side O'L.A.," *Los Angeles Times*, February 23, 1930.

9. *The Making of The Phantom of the Opera*, by Philip Riley: Page 188. Von Enger also mentions "Lon's man"—presumably Jeske.

10. Author Philip Riley has said that Chauncey Haines gave him this information many years ago. Haines, as well as anyone else who worked closely with Chaney at MGM, knew of Jeske's involvement with Chaney's make-up work. Haines said this information was kept secret out of respect for Chaney.

11. One example is "Make-up Chaney's Secret," *Los Angeles Times*, April 22, 1923. It was noted that his make-up for Quasimodo took "three hours with several people to help him."

12. J.J. Cohn to author Philip Riley and told to this author with the caveat that the comments were never meant to be published.

13. *Lon Chaney: Master Craftsman of Make Believe*, by Nathanial Ross: Page 114 – 115. Ross interviewed Creighton Chaney at the actor's home in San Clemente, California, on January 6, 1972.

14. "Lon Chaney: A Portrait of the Man Behind a Thousand Faces": *Liberty Magazine*, May 23, 1931.

15. *Lon Chaney, Jr.: Horror Film Star, 1906 – 1973*, by Don G. Smith, page 8.

16. Census workers were told Creighton's mother was born in California (Hazel's place of birth) and his birth date was moved forward to more closely match the time Lon and Hazel were married. This deception later cost Creighton some of his Social Security benefits (*Chaney: Master Craftsman of Make Believe*, by Nathanial Ross: Page 112).

17. "Chaney Departs to Study Newest Script," *Los Angeles Times*, August 11, 1925

18. Adela Rogers St. Johns from an interview with author Philip Riley.

19. "Lon Chaney: A Portrait of the Man Behind a Thousand Faces": *Liberty Magazine*, May 30, 1931.

20. "Lon Chaney: A Portrait of the Man Behind a Thousand Faces": *Liberty Magazine*, May 2, 1931. Chaney quoted Psalm 121, Verse 1: "I will lift up mine eyes unto the hills from whence cometh my help." (KJV).

21. "Lee Side O'L.A.," *Los Angeles Times*, February 23, 1930.

22. *Lon Chaney: Master Craftsman of Make Believe*, by Nathanial Ross: Page 111. Ross interviewed Creighton Chaney at the actor's home in San Clemente, California on January 6, 1972.

23. Ibid: Page 116

24. *Lon Chaney, Jr.: Horror Film Star*, 1906 – 1973, by Don G. Smith, page 91.

25. *Dark Carnival: The Secret World of Tod Browning, Hollywood's Master of the Macabre*, by David J. Skal and Elias Savada: Page 125. Chaney's non-Browning films earned an average of $30,000 more at the box office.

26. "Lon Chaney: A Portrait of the Man Behind a Thousand Faces": *Liberty Magazine*, May 30, 1931. Tod Browning also confided to St. Johns that Chaney never talked to him on the set except to say "Yes, Boss" now and then.

27. From and interview with Joan Crawford and author Philip Riley, and told to this author by Mr. Riley via email. Carnival performer Peter Dismuki was Chaney's leg double for the intricate leg work required of the armless "Alonzo" and appeared in several scenes made up as Chaney.

28. From an interview with Adela Rogers St. Johns and author Philip Riley, and told to this author by Mr. Riley via email.

29. "Lon Chaney: A Portrait of the Man Behind a Thousand Faces": *Liberty Magazine*, May 23, 1931.

30. "Mr. Chaney Studies Human Nature," *New York Times*, August 21, 1927

31. "Sign Language at Burial for Frank Chaney," *Los Angeles Times*, April 15, 1927

32. "Lon Chaney: A Portrait of the Man Behind a Thousand Faces": *Liberty Magazine*, May 30, 1931. St. Johns interviewed Hazel for her biography of Chaney—the only time Hazel ever spoke to a journalist about her late husband. It is puzzling why no one else ever tried to interview her, or possibly Hazel refused to talk to anyone but St. Johns due to her long association with the Chaney's.

33. *London After Midnight* was released the following year (1928) by publishers Grosset and Dunlap as a photoplay book edition. Authorship was credited to Marie Coolidge-Rask. This volume is extremely rare and garners a high price if found with the original dust jacket depicting an artist's rendition of a scene from the Chaney film.

34. From a conversation with author Philip Riley and told to this author via email. As with the other conversations recorded by Riley, this information was not intended for publication. Studio organist Chauncey Haines told Riley how Jeske had made the wire device used by Chaney for his eyes.

35. Linda A. Reynolds of the Inyo National Forest Service researched the deeds to the cabin and was able to find a record of Jeske's ownership. Jeske sold the cabin in 1940 to Robert and Emma Blake. In 1975 the cabin was sold to Lavina Epler and it remains in the Epler family to this date. Daniel Epler was kind enough to provide details of the interior of the cabin and photos for use in this book. It was common knowledge amongst long-time Big Pine residents that the cabin was built by Lon Chaney for John Jeske (per interviews with Kenneth Partridge; Richard Huntsberger; and "Babe" Harwood [nee' Rossi]).

36. In 2005 I asked Chaney's great-grandson, Ronald Chaney, what had happened to all the footage taken by his great-grandfather's 16mm camera. What was left of the cans of film after Lon's death eventually made their way to his son Creighton. Unfortunately, at the time of Creighton's death in

1973, Lon Jr.'s alcoholism and collection of shady friends contributed to all of the cans of film being misappropriated in some way. As of this date, no one has come forward to claim ownership of any of the Chaney 16mm film collection. Most of his still photos are also missing, but there are a handful in the Chaney family's possession. Chaney's interest in photography was noted as far back as the year 1901 when an 18-year-old Chaney took a job for the Rock Island Railroad snapping photos of the crowd who gathered in El Reno, Oklahoma, for a federal land lottery. *Harper's Weekly* correspondent William Draper covered the El Reno lottery and noted that "Chaney was a busy man taking pictures of the crowds, the trains, the land drawing, anything that looked historical. . . ." ("The Rocketing Rock Island," *Railroad Magazine*, October 1951, Vol. 56, No. 1, Page 35).

37. A home movie taken circa 1928 by Chaney's friend William Dunphy shows Chaney discussing his ideas with Dunphy's wife Mabel and Hazel in the Dunphy's backyard and showing title cards for his "production."

38. "Lon Chaney: A Portrait of the Man Behind a Thousand Faces": *Liberty Magazine*, May 23, 1931. Outside of the Feinbergs, it was Jeske who was seen the most often with Chaney around the movie studio, a fact mentioned in the 1970 article "Lon Chaney: Man of a Thousand Faces" written by DeWitt Bodeen for *Focus on Film* magazine (May-August, No. 3., page 28 – 29).

39. "Chaney and Racing King in Auto Net," *Los Angeles Times*, December 21, 1927. Race driver Peter De Paolo was the "Racing King" mentioned in the title. Both Chaney's and De Paolo's personal addresses were published in the article— something unheard of today.

40. "Make-up Now Regarded as Profession," *Los Angeles Times*, June 10, 1928. Lon Chaney was not mentioned in this article and was not a member of the new Association. Legendary

make-up artist Jack Pierce was one of the first members, along with Hugh Roman, F. B. Phillips, and others.

41. "Lon Chaney: A Portrait of the Man Behind a Thousand Faces": *Liberty Magazine*, May 30, 1931. St. Johns noted that Chaney had told his good friend, MGM publicity man Fritz Tidden, that his refusal to make a sound film was "good showmanship, even if they licked me. I wasn't one of the mob. It was news when Lon Chaney finally consented to talk."

42. "The Lon Chaney I Knew," by Clarence A. Locan: *Photoplay*, November 1930, page 60.

43. Information obtained from Answer.com: Wikipedia. Paul Revere Williams (1984 – 1980) designed over 2,000 homes for wealthy citizens of Southern California (mainly in Bel Air and Beverly Hills) and designed or was instrumental in designing many public buildings in Los Angeles.

44. "Italian Home to Have Been Lon Chaney's," *Los Angeles Times*, September 14, 1930.

45. Interview with Laura Anderson, February 17, 2005. Mrs. Anderson is mechanic Louis Mansey's niece. Mrs. Anderson said she still has a small writing desk that belonged to Hazel Chaney which was never claimed by the Chaney family after her death in 1933.

46. *Lon Chaney: Master Craftsman of Make Believe*, by Nathanial Ross: Page 199. Ross interviewed Creighton Chaney at the actor's home in San Clemente, California on January 6, 1972. Creighton claimed that his father never mentioned to him that his illness was life-threatening.

47. "Lon Chaney: A Portrait of the Man Behind a Thousand Faces," by Adela Rogers St. Johns: *Liberty Magazine*, May 30, 1931.

48. *A Thousand Faces: Lon Chaney's Unique Artistry in Motion Pictures*, by Michael Blake, page 261.

49. "Doubt Kindles Acting Fire," *Los Angeles Times*, June 9, 1929.

50. "Lon Chaney Sunburned," *Los Angeles Times*, July 21, 1929: "Permanent Make-up," *Los Angeles Times*, February 10, 1929.

51. "Oshkosh Youths Get Thrill of Lifetime—Meeting Lon Chaney," *The Daily Northwestern* (WI), March 9, 1929.

52. Ruth Biery wrote in her December 1929 article for *New Movie* magazine titled "Lon Chaney Goes Talkie" that Chaney was sent to a well-known celebrity spa in Soboda Hot Springs, California, by MGM to gain strength for his tonsillectomy. Michael Blake states on page 253 of *Lon Chaney: the Man behind the Thousand Faces* that Chaney and his wife "spent the summer months with William and Mabel Dunphy in a rented cabin at Brook Dale Lodge near Boulder Creek in the Santa Cruz mountains of Northern California." Hazel supposedly took a vacation to Hawaii with Mrs. Dunphy the same day the stock market crashed (page 254). The events leading to the crash began on October 24, 1929 and continued until the 29th, when billions of shares were cashed in. Lon and Hazel would have already been back in Los Angeles well before this time, as Chaney was scheduled to participate in a benefit circus in Beverly Hills that was to run from Friday, October 25th until Saturday, the 26th. A large number of big name Hollywood celebrities were slated to appear including Charley Chase, Laurel and Hardy, Charlie Chaplin, Joe E. Brown and many, many others. Chaney was to participate in a radio broadcast facilitated by station KEJK of Beverly Hills. It was said Chaney was one of many who "promised" to be there, but whether or not he actually attended the benefit program is not known ("Society Circus Bills Acts," *Los Angeles Times*, October 20, 1929).

53. This conversation was published in the May 30, 1931 installment of St. Johns' biography of Chaney. She notes it took place after Chaney completed his first "talkie," *The Unholy Three*, in early 1930 and he knew deep down it would be his last film.

54. "Chaney Talks!" by Harry Lang: *Photoplay*, May 1930, page 75, 141.

55. *Lon Chaney: the Man behind the Thousand Faces*, by Michael Blake, page 199 and 260.

56. "Chaney Tells How Voice is Like Make-up," *The Washington Post*, August 24, 1930.

57. "Chaney Likes New Home," *Inyo County Register*, July 12, 1930.

58. Telephone interview with Babe Harwood, June of 2005.

59. *Lon Chaney: Master Craftsman of Make Believe*, by Nathanial Ross: Page 197 – 198. Ross interviewed Creighton Chaney at the actor's home in San Clemente, California, on January 6, 1972. According to Ross, Creighton continued to believe the bleeding was a result of a botched tonsillectomy and not cancer.

60. Information obtained from Lon Chaney's Certificate of Death. Cause of death was listed by Dr. John C. Webster as "carcinoma of right lower and slight of upper bronchus" further complicated by a pulmonary hemorrhage.

61. *Love, Laughter, and Tears: My Hollywood Story*, by Adela Rogers St. Johns: Page 195.

62. "Lon Chaney: A Portrait of the Man Behind a Thousand Faces," by Adela Rogers St. Johns: *Liberty Magazine*, May 30, 1931.

63. "Hollywood Sights and Sounds," by Robbin Coons: *Key West Citizen* (FL), October 14, 1930. Mr. Coons wrote in part about actor's doubles. In regards to Chaney he said: "For actual resemblance, however, John Jeske, for years Chaney's chauffeur and best friend, is as close to a double as can be imagined. He is not in pictures, of course, but many at the Chaney funeral mistook Jeske for a brother of the star."

CHAPTER 3: A TIME OF TRAGEDY AND SORROW

1. "Lon Chaney: A Portrait of the Man Behind a Thousand Faces": *Liberty Magazine*, May 30, 1931.

2. "Lon Chaney's Former Home Reportedly Sold," *Los Angeles Times*, February 22, 1931.

3. Director Curt Siodmak made some questionable statements regarding what were confidential conversations between himself and an inebriated Creighton Chaney (then Lon Chaney, Jr.). The younger Chaney claimed to have been abused by his father, details of which Siodmak felt could not even be repeated. Siodmak was convinced Creighton was a latent homosexual. (*Lon Chaney, Jr.: Horror Film Star, 1906 – 1973*, by Don G. Smith, page 40 – 41).

4. "Lon Chaney: A Portrait of the Man Behind a Thousand Faces," by Adela Rogers St. Johns: *Liberty Magazine*, May 23, 1931. Greenwood reportedly had a talk with Creighton at Chaney's request, but, as the son replied: "That wasn't what kept me out. I wouldn't for the world have done anything Dad didn't want me to."

5. Joy had been married to a man with the surname "Puglia" back in her home state of Michigan. Mr. Puglia died sometime around the end of 1933 or January of 1934. The girls came out to California in February of 1934 to live with

their mother and stepfather. Court documents from the 1934 kidnapping trial give the daughters' names alternately as "Marie," "Myra," "Mary," "Johanna," and "Joan." Joy gave the names used in the chapter in her testimony, so I am assuming they are the correct.

6. I am in debt to Paul Beuter's stepdaughter, Laurin Peterlin, for this incredible letter, as well as photos and other materials Beuter kept from his first marriage to Grace Elaine Cadwallader.

7. "Crossing Crash Kills Motorist: Film Studio Musician Drives to Death Before Red Car," *Los Angeles Times*, August 15, 1931.

8. Information about Julius Jeske was gathered from various newspaper articles published about his death and funeral in the *Scranton Times* from November of 1931, as well as conversations with Julius' grandson, Robert Jeske.

9. "Chaney Widow's Life Ebbs," *Los Angeles Times*, October 15, 1933. Many other newspapers across the country carried this sensational story and callously spread headlines such as "Family Servant to Wed Widow of Lon Chaney" (*Chicago Daily Times*), "Lon Chaney Widow in Romance" (*Los Angeles Herald Express*), as well as other variations on that theme.

10. Ibid.

11. I have not been able to find a connection between Lynden Parker (Cora Chaney's niece Joy's husband) and Claude I. Parker, though the coincidence of the same surnames is intriguing. Claude I. Parker (1871 – 1952) had a long and colorful history as a tax attorney in Los Angeles, and was appointed by President Theodore Roosevelt as the first Collector of Internal Revenue in the 6th District in 1902. After 1913, he went into private law practice specializing in tax cases.

12. "Mrs. Lon Chaney Critically Ill," *The Lincoln Star* (NE), October 17, 1933.

13. Ibid. *The Chicago Daily Tribune, New York Times, Washington Post, Los Angeles Examiner, San Francisco Chronicle,* and other newspapers all published in October of 1933 the claim Jeske was "Lon Chaney's make-up man."

14. "Mrs. Chaney's Rites Tomorrow," *Los Angeles Times*, November 2, 1933

15. "Reveal Motives Behind Intended Chaney Marriage," *Edwardsville Intelligencer*, November 2, 1933.

16. "Chauffeur Bequeathed $25,000 by Lon Chaney's Widow," *Nevada State Journal*, Reno, NV, November 9, 1933.

17. This particular *Movie Go Round* column appeared in various newspapers across the country around November 19th through the 23rd or so, depending on the publication schedules. I could not find any commentary or a rebuttal of any kind published immediately after this column appeared, nor did I find any further articles purporting to explain the motives behind the Jeske-Chaney marriage plan.

CHAPTER 4: A CHANCE FOR HAPPINESS TURNS TO DUST:

1. The bulk of reference material for this chapter comes from legal documents such as the Jeskes' marriage license, and the careful study of court documents regarding the trial and conviction of Britton, Dorsey, Russell, Alameda, and the Parkers for the kidnapping and robbery of Jeske and his new wife. I was very fortunate to have obtained copies of most of the trial documents as well as what remains of excerpts from the closed-door Grand Jury testimony given on August 1, 1934. I was also able to comb through lengthy prison files for Britton, Dorsey, Russell, and Alameda that included personality

profiles, handwritten statements, and the story of the kidnapping in their own words. The trial testimony and Grand Jury testimony provided a fascinating, detailed look at every aspect of what led up to the kidnapping as well as a play-by-play of that horrific day itself. The events are described by a handful of individuals who all seem to have a slightly different take on what actually happened. I compiled the most repeated details to make what I believe to be a completely factual account of the events from July of 1934 and the subsequent trial and convictions.

2. The St. Regis pocket watch had been a gift from Lon Chaney.

3. Floyd Britton testified at the kidnapping trial that Elaine had been sitting on his lap for the ride back to Los Angeles.

4. "Chaney Aid is Victim of Gang: Make-up Man for Late Lon Chaney is Kidnapped by Gang," *The Newark Advocate* (OH), July 28, 1934.

5. "Movie Expert Tells How to Select Rouge," *Chicago Daily Tribune*, September 18, 1933.

6. "Mrs. Chaney Loses Gems: Home of Widow's Sister Robbed," *Los Angeles Times*, September 27, 1934: "Chaney Jewels Taken from Cache by Thief," *Los Angeles Examiner*, September 27, 1934. *The San Francisco Chronicle* reported the value of the heist to be only $7,000 ("$7,000 Jewels of Chaney Kin Stolen," September 27, 1934).

7. "Sammy Baker Seeks Girdles," *Los Angeles Times*, August 9, 1927; "Callahan Changes Plans," *Los Angeles Times*, August 11, 1927. "Mushy Callahan" was the professional name of boxer Vincent Morris Scheer (1905 – 1986), who was a Jewish newsboy from New York City. "Mushy" (it is unknown why he chose this derogatory nickname; "Callahan" was out of deference to all the great Irish boxers), spent most of his career boxing out of Southern California. After a lackluster boxing

career, a stint in the Army, and a try at running a men's clothing store, Mushy was able to parlay his boxing skills by the mid-1930s into the much more lucrative field of technical advisor for boxing scenes in the movies. Mushy later operated a gym for Warner Bros. in Hollywood.

CHAPTER 5: A LIFE IN THE SHADOWS ONCE MORE

1. "Ocean Artery Almost Ready," *Los Angeles Times*, October 17, 1926.

2. Information was obtained from the 1930 U.S. Federal Census for the 56th Assembly District. The handwriting is nearly illegible, so "Kowriak" may not be the correct spelling of Bella's last name. Her age is given as 45 years old. The waiter's name is listed as Joseph "Bolen," age 30. Again, the handwriting prevents a definitive spelling of the surname. Edward Henderson was recorded as being 65 years old in 1930.

3. "Paths Part for Victims of Kidnapping," *Los Angeles Times*, March 27, 1935; "Chaney's Old Pal Sued for Divorce," *San Francisco Chronicle*, March 28, 1935; "Court Cuts Ties of Pair in Kidnapping," *Los Angeles Times*, April 20, 1935.

4. Information regarding the Partridge family and Kenneth Partridge's memories of John Jeske were gathered from a telephone interview with Mr. Partridge on June 15, 2005 and a subsequent follow-up correspondence.

5. "Mrs. Chaney Divorces Son of Late Thespian," *Los Angeles Times*, July 25, 1935.

6. "Lawyer to Address Foreign Trade Club," *Los Angeles Times*, August 31, 1932.

7. I discovered by talking to Julius Jeske's grandson, Robert Jeske, the family never knew what happened to any of Julius'

siblings. I was at least able to find death certificates for John, Carl, and Gus and ultimately the places where they were buried to put some closure on this family's sad history.

8. "Five Fires Sweep Over Southland," *Los Angeles Times*, November 24, 1938.

9. Information on file with the Inyo National Forest Service, Bishop, California. An eccentric resident of Big Pine named Henry Kurth fooled at least one prominent Chaney biographer with stories of having known Lon Chaney. In 2005, stories were still circulating in Big Pine that Kurth used to visit Chaney at his cabin and play cards with Jeske in the evenings. He would even give presentations to the locals about his days with Chaney, et al. The truth is that Kurth did not move to the Big Pine area until around 1947 and purchased the Jeske Cabin from the Blakes' in 1952, so there is no way he could have known either Chaney or Jeske. He sold the cabin to the Epler family in 1975 and passed away in 2003.

10. Information gathered from the Los Angeles County Coroner's Register for Case #13758, File # 288.

11. Robert Jeske spoke of a potential genetic heart condition that ran on the Jeske side of his family. His sister, Audrey, for example, passed away unexpectedly and suddenly one day while gardening from a heart defect that was up to that time undetected. Without a thorough investigation of the Jeske family tree, it will be impossible to pinpoint exactly the nature of the defect. Unfortunately, the family is very disconnected and without much of its written history, so it is unlikely any such definitive diagnosis will ever be made.

12. The Los Angeles County Coroner's Register documents a man named Walter R. Powers, an associate of Ralph W. Smith's law firm, appeared at the coroner's office on August 8, 1944 to pick up Jeske's personal belongings. He is listed on the

Register as being a "Rep for Bro." No further details are given in this document. Robert Jeske said there was a family story that had been handed down to him about Gus Jeske receiving a large amount of cash and a car after John's death. Since John died without a will and his estate was not probated until 1948—a year after Gus' death—it is most likely the gifts in question were given by John during his lifetime.

EPILOGUE

1. Information gathered from court documents and tax records filed in Los Angeles and El Dorado County. Information on George Dorsey was taken from his prison file. Gus Jeske's information was gathered from his Certificate of Death and the Letters of Administration filed by Catherine Dworczak. Catherine's husband Henry Dworczak used to live in the home on Prospect Avenue in Scranton, PA, where Gus had a room prior to his marriage (Henry and Catherine set up house just down the street). His father, Joseph, was a funeral director and Henry learned the trade from him. The letters from Elaine to Paul Beuter were graciously copied for me by Beuter's daughter, Laurin Peterlin.

2. *Lon Chaney, Jr.: Horror Film Star, 1906 – 1973*, by Don G. Smith, page 103.

Appendix I

Amongst her stepfather's belongings, Laurin Peterlin was able to find a handwritten love letter from July 10th of 1927 that had been saved by Paul Beuter, Grace Elaine Cadwallader's first husband. What was so remarkable about this love letter is that it had been written by some unknown lover to his wife Elaine shortly after the couple had moved from Hollywood to San Francisco. Laurin was kind enough to allow me to handle the original letter. What struck me immediately is the similarity of the handwriting to what I have collected of John Jeske's handwriting. I thought it would be such a thrilling find to prove the author of this passionate letter was indeed Jeske, and he had met Elaine earlier than I had at first believed.

In April of 2005 I contacted a renowned handwriting analyst, Ronald N. Morris, who graciously agreed to look over the letter and samples of Jeske's known handwriting (mainly signatures—the largest sample was from the 1941 Social Security application) to see if there was indeed a match. I sent him high-quality scans of all the materials and before too long he sent back his reply. It is his professional opinion that the writer of the 1927 love letter was not Jeske, but left the door open just a crack by saying it may be worthwhile to conduct another examination if more extensive samples of Jeske's handwriting could be found. The letter's author gives the distinct impression of being a foreign born person who could speak English well, but had a very shaky grasp of English grammar and punctuation. Even if Jeske did not write it, the letter provides a fascinating glimpse into Elaine's complex and tantalizing world:

Dearest

Just got back from the beach had a early morning swim all by myself got home and your sweet letter was pushed below the door how glad I was to hear from you. Well dearest your letter gives me a tinge of regret. You say you are a model of virtue in San Francisco, did I change you in Hollywood, to me you were always a good girl. Your purity and duty always stood out to me above everything else my love for you was the sweetest thing that ever came in to my life, you have it and no one can take it from you our passions we may never know the wonderful Joy of it again but my love be always for you no one can ever arouse passion in me I am like you in that respect you say in your letters your duty to Paul comes first. Those are the traits in you that I admire, my soul cries out in agony for you and my heart is very sad to day, the want of you not being here; but you say ask God to guide us I have done that and I feel that you are lost to me; to me. Oh Elaine it is hard for [me] to write this to you, because I am beginning to view the hopeless side of ever being able to call you mine I had dreamed that the near future we would be happy together and write and create a happy love for you and I, but I plainly see in all your letters your duty to Paul comes first he has the moral right to you at all times. Oh dearest I cannot write to you anymore my heart is in anguish, each day I get a letter from you I want you more than ever and I see that I can not have you without causing grief to you and every one else Oh God I wish you were not married and that you were free to come to me. Oh dearest my mind is tortured with the thoughts of never having those wonderful happy times together again I wish I were dead; the only comfort I have is knowing I gave you my love to keep and that I have yours. Dearest the days are long and the nights are a thousand years I wake up and say Elaine dear I love you I love you and you are a long way from me and can not hear me say those words. Oh dearest I am like a baby crying for the things It cannot have, why is it the fates are so cruel to us we love one another I could cheat the fates by ending it all, but I would not spoil our love to have such a stain upon us and I am stronger in mind for too think of such an act, dearest forgive me for this letter you ask to write but I feel and I am doing so, I am willing to do anything you say to make you and I happy I would gladly give my life for you knowing I made you happy and successful these are all the things I live for; you and your writing your success will be mine my reward to make you happy.

I love you always

Bibliography

BOOKS:

Ackerman, Forrest J. *Lon of 1000 Faces!* California: Morrison, Raven-Hill Company, 1983

Anderson, Robert G. *Faces, Forms, Films: The Artistry of Lon Chaney.* New York: Castle Books, 1971.

Biscailuz, Eugene W.; Bynum, Lindley; and Jones, Idwal. *Biscailuz: Sheriff of the New West.* New York: Morrow, 1950.

Blake, Michael F. *Lon Chaney: The Man Behind the Thousand Faces.* Maryland: The Vestal Press, 1990, 1993.

_____. *A Thousand Faces: Lon Chaney's Unique Artistry in Motion Pictures*: New York: The Vestal Press, 1995.

Conner, Floyd. *Lupe Velez and Her Lovers.* New York: Barricade Books, Inc., 1993.

Riley, Philip J. *A Blind Bargain: Ackerman Archives Series Volume II.* New Jersey: MagicImage Filmbooks, 1988

_____. *The Phantom of the Opera: Classic Silents, Volume 1.* New Jersey: MagicImage Filmbooks, 1999

Ross, Nathaniel Lester. *Lon Chaney: Master Craftsman of Make Believe.* (Self-published: Quality RJ, 1981, 1988)

St. Johns, Adele Rogers. *Love, Laughter, and Tears: My Hollywood Story.* New York: Doubleday and Company, Inc., 1978: Signet-New American Library, 1979.

____. *The Honeycomb.* New York: Doubleday and Company, Inc., 1969.

Skal, David J. and Savada, Elias. *Dark Carnival: The Secret World of Tod Browning, Hollywood's Master of the Macabre.* New York: Anchor Books, 1995.

Smith, Don G. *Lon Chaney, Jr.: Horror Film Star, 1906 – 1973.* North Carolina: McFarland & Company, Inc., 1996.

MAGAZINE AND NEWSPAPER ARTICLES:

Over a hundred newspaper and magazine articles from large and small sources across the country were reviewed during my research phase and the most significant of these have been cited in the Endnotes. Due to the large volume of articles, it is not possible to cite them all.

TELEPHONE INTERVIEWS:

Freda Hollenback (John Jeske's niece), Scranton, PA: September 10, 2004

Alice Brink (John Jeske's niece), Sunnyside, CA: October 18, 2004

Laura Anderson (Louis and Ona Mansey's niece), Seattle, WA: February 17, 2005

Dick Hunstberger (spent summers in Big Pine at the family cabin as a kid. Knew Ruluff Slimmer and stories about Jeske's cabin), Camarillo, CA: March 29, 2005

George "Ted" Hunstsberger (Dick's older brother), Cedar Cress, NM: March 29, 2005

Babe (Rossi) Harwood, Big Pine, CA: March 30, 2005

Kenneth Partridge, Bishop, CA: June 15, 2005

Robert Jeske (John Jeske's grand-nephew), PA: I spoke to Bob on the phone and via email so many times I am unable to list them all. Needless to say, he provided a great deal of help and encouragement.

COURT DOCUMENTS:

The bulk of my research centered on legal documents, each one opening the door to a deeper mystery. I obtained last wills and testaments for Lon Chaney and Hazel Chaney, as well as a huge file of documents covering Hazel's lengthy probate proceedings from shortly after her death in 1933 until 1938. John Jeske's certificate of death was obtained as well as the file dealing with his 1948 probate proceedings and other files regarding Lon, Jr.'s suit to obtain title to the Placerville, CA property, marriage license, divorce documents, various bills of sales and other documents regarding his attempt to purchase the Alturas Hotel business, Social Security application, all immigration and naturalization documents, ship manifests from his voyage to America, voter registration records, and phone directory information. Certificates of death were obtained for the Jeske brothers Julius, Karl, and Gustav (I also found probate documents for Gus), as well as for Grace Elaine Cadwallader (Beuter, Jeske, Montgomery, D'Aguino, Johnson), two of her husbands, and many others involved in the Jeske story. Property documents were also located for Elaine and her mother's real estate deal in 1936 and Jeske's sale of his inherited property in 1938 and 1940.

Index

CPSIA information can be obtained
at www.ICGtesting.com
Printed in the USA
BVHW042023120620
581231BV00006B/177

9 781593 933302